HEAVEN'S POINT GUARD

HEAVEN'S POINT GUARD

The Kirk Gentrup Story

Ken "Cruiser" Gentrup
Shaun C. Kilgore

FOUNDERS HOUSE PUBLISHING

HEAVEN'S POINT GUARD: The Kirk Gentrup Story

First edition, November 2010
Published by Founders House Publishing, LLC
www.foundershousepublishing.com

ISBN: 978-0-9843764-1-4

Cover and interior design by Shaun C. Kilgore
www.shaunkilgore.com

Printed in the United States of America

This book is dedicated to Kirk and to all of my family, friends, and to the many people who knew and loved my son.

~ Cruiser

I dedicate this book to my family, friends, and everyone else who was encouraged with my involvement in bringing Kirk's story to print. Thank you all.

~ Shaun

ACKNOWLEDGEMENTS

I want to take the opportunity to recognize the many people who offered support, comfort, and assistance in the aftermath of Kirk's death. There have been so many over the years that I cannot begin to list all of them. I don't want to name individuals because that would take more space than this book provides. Instead let me offer sincere thanks to several groups.

To all of Kirk's teammates and coaches in AAU Y Ball, Little League, and at North Vermillion High School, I thank you.

To those who gave at the auctions, the golf outings, and other events for the scholarship fund, I thank you.

To those who were there for us before, during, and after the funeral, I thank you. We were all humbled by the outpouring of love and compassion during the loss of Kirk.

To this day, we are deeply appreciative of the care we receive from people we cross paths with each day.

Kirk was a special kid, but only because each and every one of you made him that way. His memory will be kept alive forever because of many special people.

CONTENTS

FOREWORD

I met Ken "Cruiser" Gentrup for the first time after I called him to discuss the prospect of putting together a book about his son Kirk Gentrup, a 16-year-old boy who was fatally struck by lightning on a baseball field in 1995. I had heard of Cruiser and certainly knew about Kirk. I was a local. If Kirk would have been born a matter of months earlier he would have been a member of my graduating class. I shared the halls with Kirk. I don't recall having classes with him; you might chalk that up to a faulty memory on my part. Still, I remember his smile and his wit. I cannot say I was close to him as so many others were. Certainly, Kirk had his share of intimate friends and associations, but he also had the charisma and personality to attract a broader group of people who numbered themselves as his friends. As I worked on this book, I quickly discovered how true this was.

The inside story of his death and the effects of this tragedy on Ken and the rest of Kirk's family were unknown to me. The emotions and the grief and acceptance that cascaded through the North Vermillion School Corporation, even to the surrounding communities on both sides of the state line, onward even to southern Indiana and beyond. At the time, the full impact was not clear to me. It is only as I was reintroduced to Kirk's story, through the many aspects which were conveyed in Ken's words, that I really grasped its extent—perhaps I still am.

The book that Ken wished to write was more than an account of Kirk's untimely death. He wanted to present a picture of Kirk's life, his accomplishments, and his sheer talent and determination as an individual and an athlete. It was his way of ensuring Kirk's legacy—another step to preserve the story like the creation of the Kirk Gentrup Memorial Scholarship.

With that in mind, I was able to provide a blend of Ken's memories of Kirk, many of them childhood stories, along with a very sobering account of that narrow window of time in which Kirk was killed. It carried on through the outpouring of support, the community response, through the visitation and, finally, the funeral. As Ken put it, it was "Four Days of Hell."

Following that account, I included the eulogy that was given at the funeral and a letter that Ken wrote to Kirk. Letters and other messages from Kirk's friends and some compassionate strangers who were affected by Kirk's death make up the content of the next chapter. Other stories about Kirk and highlights of Ken's own efforts to deal with the loss of his son follow. A whole chapter is devoted to Kirk's home away from home, the gymnasium where he spent countless hours working on his basketball skills. The final chapter, "Time Marches On," seemed a good place to end the narrative of Ken's story—even though, it was clear that it wasn't really the end. *Heaven's Point Guard* is a new chapter in Kirk's story.

For me this was more than an opportunity to publish a second book, it was a chance to give something back to the community where I was raised and spent most of my life. My role as co-author was to develop Ken's notes into a cohesive book. I hope that I've accomplished that task.

Shaun Kilgore
Danville, IL
2010

A TRIBUTE TO KIRK

By Donna Dunham

A boy was sent from Heaven.
We had him sixteen years.
Then God called him home again,
'Midst tragedy and tears.

He was one of the finest people
That God had ever made.
His name was Kirk, our pride and joy,
His memories will not fade.

Kirk always wore the brightest smile –
His eyes lit up with joy.
Everyone that met him,
Loved our little boy.

The lives he touched in those short years
Are too numerous to recall.
But they will not forget him –
They loved him one and all.

Kirk was destined to play basketball.
From day one it was his sport.
With his quick and natural talent,
He was a challenge on the court.

His head coach, now, is our own God –
He plays basketball every day.
"The best point guard they've ever seen"
Is what the angels say.

"Never give up! Continue!"
Kirk would tell us here today.
He'll be our guide through every hour –
And in our hearts he'll stay.

We'll miss him daily with all our hearts
This young man that we love.
But we'll feel him looking down on us
From his place in Heaven, above.

Ken "Cruiser" Gentrup and Kirk Gentrup

INTRODUCTION

Remembering Kirk

Today is April 8, 2010—just another day to most of you. People don't comment on the passage of a day unless there is a reason. Most days pass by without us paying attention. Dates only have a deeper meaning when we recognize that something important or memorable happened on those days. Anniversaries, weddings, birthdays, holidays, and other occasions are great examples of this. History itself is often summed up by the dates on which formative or dramatic events occurred. I'm sure many people can remember where they were or what they were doing on such occasions. As it is with times of celebration and achievement, so it is with tragedies.

Those old enough to remember may recall the assassination of President John F. Kennedy. For some people—even after forty-seven years—each moment of that fateful day remains crystal clear, the details sharp and distinctive. Who today can read the date "September 11th" without thinking of those terrible events at the World Trade Center in 2001? I'm sure many of you can think of a thousand other times in your life when the terrible and the unexpected happened. Sometimes, an event has identifiable causes—in these cases, the actions of people. Other times, you are left without an answer for why those events truly happened. It is an unaccountable mystery, a seemingly random act of nature. Call it an act of God, call it coincidence, call it what you will, such experiences as these offer little in the way of comfort and no easy answers. Tragedies are easier to remember because they are so shocking, so unexpected. No matter how much time has passed it may still be like they just happened. When a tragedy occurs on such a scope, the effects can be far-reaching and unexpected. It makes no difference whether it is something of national significance or if its impact centers in some small town across America. Lives are irrevocably changed.

For me, April 8th is a day I will never forget, a day etched into my memory. You see, on April 8, 1995 my son Kirk was struck and killed by lightning during a high school baseball game. It has been fifteen years. Fifteen years since the day that changed the rest of my life—and lives of countless others. I knew then that I would write about him someday. I just didn't know it would take this long. Part of the challenge that comes with writing a book like this is to have some notion about what I wanted to say. I know that there are reasons, some personal and some that have more to do with the responsibility I believe I have to share Kirk's story. I feel I must offer this book as another way to keep his memory alive and, hopefully, share his life with others. Let me try to explain.

KINDLING HIS MEMORY

My family and I were motivated by a personal need to use Kirk's death to produce positive results. It was for this purpose that the Kirk Gentrup Scholarship Fund was created in the first place. We've had many benefits to raise money for the fund and dedicated many hours to preserving this resource for generations to come. We have over $100,000 in his scholarship endowment. More than $80,000 has been awarded to students in his name. There is an annual golf outing that is held in Kirk's honor. The course is always filled and people look forward to playing it. It has become like a reunion for Kirk's family and friends. It is competitive, but fun, just as Kirk was in his life. Additionally, for many years, we had auctions that included around one hundred items that were put up for sale. Even today, we still receive occasional donations in Kirk's name, as part of other benefits and activities held throughout the area. These have all been great tools to keep Kirk's name relevant and familiar.

Yet, after fifteen years, Kirk's generation has passed through school and many of the students now receiving his scholarship know less and less about him as a person. This fact is one of the primary reasons that I've decided to tell this story. It is a way to prevent his memory from slipping away. The book is a reminder to them of who he was, what he stood for, and the dedication he demonstrated. Kirk was a tremendous example.

He has been much of my inspiration since his untimely death. I was lucky enough to have coached a girls' state champion basketball team in 2002 and we were runners-up the following year. Kirk was always the example I used when instructing the girls. In many cases, the girls knew Kirk when they were still in grade school. As I hope to show more than once throughout this book, Kirk possessed a fierce work ethic, dedication, a talent for fundamentals, and just about any other aspect of the game you could imagine. Following every tournament we won I took a piece of the net to his grave and thanked him for the inspiration he gave me. I remember when he played I always made sure he was kind to the younger kids who looked up to him.

I tried to instill this same manner into my girls' teams. As state champions they were really idolized a lot by those young and upcoming players. I told them to always cut two pieces of net and give one to those waiting children. I considered each piece a symbol of inspiration and encouragement. I believe that you must seize these opportunities because they may not come along very often. As my grandchildren could tell you, Kirk's memory and accomplishments are cherished and he lives as a guiding example for anyone who desires to know something about dedication and perseverance in athletics—and life.

HOPE AND COMFORT

Kirk's story has become my story. I've devoted pages of notes on my thoughts and feelings over the years. By writing this, I am sharing my personal pain and detailing my thoughts and my attempts to come to grips with Kirk's death. In a way, I hope this book can offer some comfort to those people who have lost children.

The thoughts and insights I've gained may offer them the means to cope with the grief and sadness that comes from such deep and personal tragedy. I don't believe there is anything harder than dealing with a child's death. If there is, I haven't experienced it and I hope I never do. The idea of a parent losing a child is so unnatural, so disturbing, especially under such circumstances.

Thankfully, in many ways, both my family and I have been able to move on with our lives. I am blessed with healthy, smart, athletic grandchildren and this takes up so much of our time. Our grandchildren know who Kirk is and what kind of person he was. They can all tell you a lot about him. It's almost like they know him personally.

He's not here physically but he is very much here emotionally, mentally, and yes, spiritually. I don't think very many people who knew Kirk can look at Diana or me and not think about Kirk. His life (and his death) left an indelible mark on everyone he knew. The means to measure his life's impact on others is rooted in the special circumstances of his death. What could be more calculated to draw the attention of the public than something like a lightning strike? There is another level of significance there.

What kind of life Kirk would have led is left to the imagination. He was well on his way to being a great basketball player, possibly the best or one of the best to come out of North Vermillion High School. He was on track to becoming the all-time leading scorer. He had already won several major awards as a freshman and a sophomore. He was leading the baseball team in batting average when he was struck down. He had the admiration of his friends, many of whom told me that they believed he was immortal. The truth is that Kirk was simply a good kid, not perfect, but a decent person and a fine athlete. Most of all, I believe my son was a good Christian.

There is some added comfort in this last point. It was the source of our hope and strength once our family had lost Kirk. He was baptized and he believed in God. In fact, there were certain facts about Kirk's faith that we did not learn about until after he was gone. When cleaning out his bedroom, we found that he had written extensively in his bible. He wrote down passages from the scriptures and included many of his own thoughts about God and the faith.

Knowing how he believed in and how he felt about God certainly remains a comfort even today. Kirk taught us all a lesson, even in his death. Each of us was left with much to think about and imagine. We know in our hearts that Kirk is now dwelling with Christ. It is the bedrock of this belief that has helped to sustain me over the years: I will see my son again. We will all be reunited some day.

There have been times where I would have rather left this earth sooner so I could be with him, but time has done its part to heal those wounds, though the scars remain. I've had to trust that what God had in mind for Kirk was far better than what any of us, even Kirk, would have chosen. I am thankful that God allowed Kirk's mother, Diana, and I to have such a son, if only for a short time. When Diana and I stood by his casket for the last time, I'll never forget her words: "I knew he wouldn't be here long; he was too good to be true."

* * *

I always thought that my Kirk was a pretty special boy. I think all fathers should feel this way. There is something wrong with any father who doesn't. I don't think, even for a minute, that Kirk was any more special than any other child. Every child is special in their own way, whether it is athletically, scholastically, or maybe in music, spirituality, or something else. In a parent's eyes every child should be special in his or her own way. But we, as a family, will always think that the way Kirk was taken and the events surrounding his death and the lives he touched, makes his death most unusual. He touched far many more lives than we had ever dreamed. I think God made him for a particular reason because of the way all these events took place. I think the newspapers and television made it special because of all the publicity surrounding it.

Here is the way I personally look at what happened. God wanted an angel, a special angel for special duties. When picking this angel he wanted to wake up a lot of people spiritually. So it had to be someone who had touched many lives. God chose Kirk. I've been told that the word "angel" means messenger. Certainly, one could argue that Kirk was in a unique position to be a messenger. His life and his death were the substance of the messages that God wanted to share.

Kirk was smart, popular, and was looked up to by both children and adults. God wanted this to have an impact on this community as well as the surrounding communities. Believe me when I say it had a tremendous impact! Kirk had done more and touch more lives in his sixteen years on this earth than many do in a full lifetime. (I still feel that the tremendous growth in a local church coincided with Kirk's death. I know several of his friends got baptized shortly after his death.) Yes, God chose Kirk, and as time goes on I can see more and more reasons why Kirk was chosen. I know I'll never totally understand why, but I have learned to accept it more every day. It just seemed that he had set such high goals and he had so much more to do here on earth, but I guess there were better things waiting in the next life.

* * *

I remember watching television one night and Tommy Lasorda (then the manager of the Los Angeles Dodgers) was on ESPN with Roy Firestone. Lasorda was asked about the son he had lost recently. He said he had a lot of trouble dealing with it until one day a friend asked him that if thirty-six years ago God would have given him a choice to not have had his son at all, or to have had his son for the thirty-six years and then take him away. Tommy said that most definitely he would take him, knowing that in thirty-six years he would lose him back to God. He said he wouldn't give up the memories for anything.

That's the way I feel about Kirk. If God had given me the same choice, without a moment of hesitation, I would have said yes Even if it was only for sixteen years, I would have said yes. I wouldn't trade the memories for anything! In my mind, God gave Kirk such a wonderful life that we could all enjoy and, if you will, God gave Kirk what I think of as a glorified death, one that no one will ever forget. His death, it seemed, was almost as special as his life, maybe even more so.

SHARING THE TRUTH

When Kirk was taken from us I was there. I was staring directly at him when it happened. For that reason I felt the need to offer an account of those events. I don't want any horror stories about what took place on that baseball field. In fact, I started writing down those events very shortly after they happened.

Now, fifteen years later, I felt like it was time to prepare this book. I think that I have gone over, revised, and reexamined these events as much as I can. I've taken them as far as I can on my own. In order to bring this book into being, I sought out a writer to help put my words in a more polished form. Together, I hope we can present Kirk's story clearly and faithfully. I remember throughout the events following Kirk's death that whenever the newspaper or television stations called I tried to cooperate with them. I was uncompromising in my desire to present everything as accurately as possible. I was rather tough on a few of them. Again, I was there. I know what happened. I saw what happened. I didn't want anyone to assume anything. Kirk's mother and I wanted positive things to come out of this. So we wanted everything to be only the truth—no hearsay. The publicity of Kirk's death was vast, but also very respectful. I thanked the newspapers and television for being so kind, caring, and considerate.

This book is a chance to set the record straight and tell my son's story. It is an opportunity to reach out to those who knew him, cherished his love and friendship, and remember him fondly today. In the following pages, I will share both Kirk's life and the events of his death. I will do my best to offer you a portrait of a brilliant and gifted young man that left us far too soon. I also wish to share what I and many others have done to bring good things from something so terrible. This is my journey as much as it is his. This is a testimony about how Kirk's life changed mine.

CHAPTER ONE

A Small Town Boy

"He was a friend you could talk to, laugh with, and cry with. Now, I cry with others for the one friend who could marvel you with his mind, his dreams, and his skills. As a basketball player he could shoot like Bird, dazzle you like Jordan, and pass like Stockton. He had a heart like a lion."

~ Jason Cardwell

My son, Kirk Alan Gentrup, was born on December 13, 1978. He was named after a friend and neighbor of ours named Morris Kirchoff, a painting contractor that I had worked for during high school and throughout college and whom I had grown to admire. I'm not sure when I started calling him "Kirk," but that nickname was given a whole new meaning when my son was born. I liked the name and it was so different than the other names that were popular at that time. Diana and I felt that it fit our newborn son well.

There was nothing unusual about Kirk's upbringing, nothing in his background to suggest that he would be any more exceptional than any other child. In many ways, Kirk was a just another small town boy, living in rural Indiana. Yet, he did stand out. Early on, Kirk discovered sports and found something he loved, especially when it came to basketball. I can't say that this was a big surprise. After all, I, myself, considered basketball my "first love." Both as a player and later as a coach, I remained immersed in it. However, without question, my attachment to the game paled in comparison to Kirk's passion and love of it. He ate, drank, and slept basketball.

EARLY MEMORIES

I remember coming into his room at night while he slept just to watch him sleep. I often wondered what his dreams might be about. Like anyone had to wonder. Kirk was probably dreaming of basketball! Every free moment Kirk was playing, watching, or studying the game. Countless hours were spent improving his performance. Kirk realized early on, when he was young, that he would not grow much taller than 6′1″ or 6′2″ at the most. He understood that he would need to work that much harder to master all the skills of the game, especially ball handling.

There was particular event that showcased my son's determination to excel regardless of any perceived limitations (such as height) that may have stopped other kids. If I remember right, he was in either the second or third grade. Even back then he often told me that he was going to be the best point guard to ever play college basketball. Kirk, like other kids, set lofty goals, but he took the crucial step to do the work necessary to make such fantasies more like realities. (Honestly, I believe he was well on his way to this goal at the time of his death.)

I will never forget something he told me once. He said, "Dad, when we warm up before the games, I'm not going to be embarrassed. I'm going to dunk just like the big guys."

Not content with mere words, Kirk went into action. When he was older, Kirk worked hours with strength shoes, jumping rope, and other things to increase his leaping ability. Before he died at 5'9" as a high school sophomore, Kirk could dunk the ball. I'll never forget how happy that made him.

During that same period, when he was in elementary school, his mother brought home an exercise trampoline. Kirk had his own goal out in the driveway plus numerous goals throughout the house and garage. However, Kirk wasn't content to dunk on his mini-goals. He wanted to dunk on a real goal—a ten-foot regulation goal. So Kirk got out his mother's trampoline and took off running and jumped off the trampoline to dunk the ball. His face went up into the net and his two front teeth became entangled. One tooth was pulled out and the other left hanging. Luckily, he wasn't hurt worse since he landed back first. He went into the house all bloody to show his mother what he had done.

She found the tooth and rushed him to the dentist. The tooth was put back in, the other straightened. The teeth were bonded to the others. These were his permanent teeth so it was very important that this bonding worked. Although he would later wear braces, the teeth turned out to be all right and Kirk always had a beautiful smile.

Kirk later told me, "Man. That really hurt Dad, but I just wanted to dunk." Looking back, that episode now seems funny but at the time we were grateful that Kirk wasn't hurt worse.

* * *

When Kirk was about five years old—just the height of the bathroom sink—he was standing there watching me shave. I used put shaving cream on his face and shave him. Of course, I held the razor backwards, but he didn't know. Kirk was standing there waiting for me to shave him when he suddenly sneezed. He jerked his head forward and hit the corner of the sink. The edge punctured his head just above the eye. Needless to say, he bled like stuck hog. I got a towel over the cut and rushed him to the hospital. He didn't cry a lot but I'll never forget his reaction on the way. As he whimpered tiny little tears he kept asking, "Dad, am I going to die." I said, "No Kirk, probably just a few stitches."

When we arrived, I'll never forget how I was treated. They started questioning me about how this had happened. When I told them, it was like they didn't believe me. I have to admit it was a strange accident but when Kirk told them they believed him. If only they knew how I felt about this little boy (my Kirk) they would have never bothered to ask. I think I was one of those parents who feel the pain worse than the child when they get hurt. I can remember saying many times that it hurt me worse than it hurt them. (I think when Kirk died I died right along with him. Only mine is a longer lasting, slower type of death that goes on every day. I've had many people tell me, especially my ballplayers, that when Kirk died it was like I died too. I know a big part of me, of all of us, went along with him.)

* * *

The first coach to ever take Kirk under his wing was Coach Brian Hughes. When Coach Hughes had his camp in the summer for grades 3-8 he called to see if Kirk could attend. We told him Kirk would only be in the first grade. Coach Hughes said he wanted Kirk there anyway. Kirk went and ended up winning the camp's free throw award. Coach Hughes said he could have won other awards too but he thought it wouldn't be fair to the other kids. I agreed and knew Kirk would have agreed also.

At least, Coach Hughes said, the free throws are there in the numbers and there should be no argument. But some parents did voice their complaints, some saying that Kirk shouldn't have been there because of his age. Kirk proceeded to win the free throw award every year after that up until the time of his death.

* * *

During Kirk's sixth grade season I was watching a game against Fountain Central. Kirk played wonderfully and ended up with 29 points. After the game a man came up to me and asked if I was Kirk's father. He introduced himself as Jim Robinson, a former coach at Fountain Central who had been there when I was playing for North Vermillion.

Mr. Robinson told me that Kirk was the best he'd ever seen at that age. He said he had such a complete game. He just loved watching him play. Later that year Bernard Gideon, a longtime coach at Montezuma handed Kirk the same compliment at a sixth grade tournament. I'll never forget one moment during this tournament. There were a few seconds left in the half and someone threw Kirk the ball and Kirk looked at the clock, looked at the three point line, saw he was on the line, took one dribble backwards and hit a three point shot at the buzzer. Mr. Gideon told me he was amazed that a kid would have that kind of understanding of the game at that age. This particular tournament meant a lot to Kirk because the year before his team had lost in this final in three overtimes after Kirk had fouled out. He told me then that they would win next year and they did.

When someone hands you a compliment about your son, it means a lot, but when one comes from a coach, such praise means more because they see more and understand more than just the scoring aspect of the game. They have the eyes to see the subtler points of performance and technique.

A MODEST STAR

There was nothing that made me prouder of my son than the simple fact that despite all of native talent and exceptional abilities, he was a rather modest person. It was something I think others understood as well. I, as a father, remember all those good things and I was often so proud I felt like I would bust at the seams. I've come to realize that I probably talked more about Kirk's exploits than he ever did.

When I stop to consider all of the instances where Kirk displayed his deep modesty and humility, I'm not sure where to begin. I remember a time in grade school when his team won a game 25-21 in which Kirk scored every point. It was a proud moment for me but I don't think he ever mentioned it. I think some people in that gymnasium may more easily recall how the "big star" would come up in the bleachers after a game and sit on my lap and give me a hug and a kiss. (I know I will never forget those hugs and kisses.)

Later, during his seventh grade year, I remember a game against Covington. We were the away team playing at the home court of our "bitter rival." Of course, I doubt those seventh graders took the rivalry so seriously. However, I think this game meant a bit more to Kirk since many of the players on the opposing team were the same kids he had played little league baseball with in the past. Also, the previous year, Covington had inflicted the only loss of the season against Kirk's team.

Kirk and I had talked about this game long before it came about, so I knew Kirk would be pretty pumped up for the game. The game ended up being rather close throughout but in the end we won. Afterwards, I scanned the scorebook, as I always did, to see how we did at the free throw line as opposed to our opponents. I've always been a firm believer that many games are won or lost at the free throw line. Also Kirk and I had this little ritual. Basically, after every game whether he was playing or I was playing we would tell the other how many free throws were missed. When looking in the book I was astonished to see Kirk had shot twenty free throws and made nineteen. That's ninety-five percent, an unbelievable performance.

Do you know what he said when I walked into the locker room?

"I know dad, I missed a free throw." All I could do was smile and go over and give him a big hug and tell him how proud I was.

When I figured our stats at the end of our first season, Kirk's seventh grade year, I was surprised at one particular stat: total points. Kirk had led our team in scoring with 275 points and the next closest was a total of 54. When seeing this stat most people would automatically think Kirk was a ball hog, but this wasn't the case at all. I remember urging him to shoot more than he did but Kirk was always so unselfish. He averaged only eleven shots a game and generally averaged twenty points each time. I think he preferred to give the other players the opportunity to score. He took more satisfaction out of an assist than he did scoring himself. He proved this later in his career when he won the assists awards in both his freshman and sophomore years on the varsity team. He took a lot of pride in his assists and free throw shooting.

Even Kirk's coaches wanted him to shoot more, but I think he was smarter than the rest of us. He knew that the other kids needed a chance to score if they would ever be any good at the game. He worked to make his teammates the best they could be. He was always encouraging them. Kirk had the sort of dedication or that drive that some of his teammates lacked or failed to cultivate.

Let me put it this way: Whenever there was a school dance following a game, the rest of the players would clean up and go over to the cafeteria. Kirk, on the other hand, would go back to the gym and work on his game. I would see kids looking through the windows into the gym staring Kirk like he was nuts. They couldn't understand why he would rather be shooting hoops than spending time with girls at the dance. Some said he must be crazy. But, he loved basketball that much. It was his number one priority. Kirk never made a big deal out of his commitment to basketball; he just refused to be turned aside from it by anything.

His pursuit of excellence was one entirely centered on the game. At the same time, he was never one to seek glory or recognition. I think I've shown that much by noting Kirk's actions on the court. He had the sort of single-minded determination that can make anything seem possible. As a student he did well enough, but he wasn't after academic honors or accolades. Kirk managed A's and B's and was fine with that.

When it came to things like running for class office he never had much interest unless someone talked him into running. Of course, this seldom happened. Kirk had a few reasons why he felt the need to decline such offers. One reason was that he was afraid that such duties might take away time he could be spending on the court. He was also worried that some would feel he was sending the message that he believed he was better than someone else. Kirk never felt that way. He didn't want to deny anyone an opportunity. When he was nominated homecoming attendant or something like that, he always reacted with embarrassment.

I think that many times, Kirk was too modest. Despite his sense of fairness to his fellow players and the lack of interest he took in the everyday details of the game like his stats, Kirk did have sincere desire to be a standout in basketball. He worked and worked to perform the best. He wanted to be Kirk, great basketball player. This desire was always slightly at odds with his interest in the accomplishments of the whole group—or at least other people.

VARSITY PLAY

Kirk's freshman year we all knew he would play varsity basketball. He had just worked too hard for this, ever since before he started school. Coach Mark Atherton however had decided not to throw him in the fire. He would bring him along slowly. For five games Kirk played junior varsity for two quarters and then he would switch to varsity for two quarters. Kirk never really liked this arrangement because he wasn't able to get comfortable in either game.

The varsity team had a bad start to the season and after only five games Coach Atherton resigned. Following this, Kirk Booe took over as varsity coach. The first thing he did was move Kirk up to play varsity full-time. Our first game under Coach Booe was at Turkey Run and even though

Kirk didn't start he was inserted into the game about three minutes into the first quarter. Kirk went in and played like a seasoned veteran. He handled Turkey Run's full court press very well, had several assists, and contributed sixteen points.

It was plain to see that Kirk was there to stay. Even though we didn't win many games, many came down to the wire. Game attendance increased and many people went just to watch Kirk. Perhaps, I'm a bit prejudiced but Kirk was a fun and exciting player to watch. Throughout his time on the court, the attendance stayed up. The season after he died many people commented on how low attendance was at the games.

After his first full varsity game Kirk never talked about what a good game he had played. He wasn't mad because they lost. He was upset because many of the players didn't seem to care that they had lost. It was a disturbing experience for Kirk. He had always enjoyed playing on his AAU team because all the players shared a larger measure of his dedication and they had a hunger to win. Kirk's first varsity game was a success for him but not for the team and that bothered him. Everyone started talking about this promising freshman from North Vermillion but his main concern was for the team and that was the way it always was with him. He never talked of individual records but of team accomplishment like winning the conference or sectional. I still believe that if the older kids would have let him, Kirk would have led them to many more victories. He had a heart for teamwork and collective accomplishment. Such attitudes shone brightly as characteristics of pure leadership.

TAKE KIRK OUT – NO WAY!

Kirk's presence on the court was something that did not go undisputed. I think this was especially true during his seventh grade season. During this period, I was the basketball coach so there were some voices that suggested I was playing favorites since my son was playing so often. This undercurrent came to a head for me during a game against Fountain Central.

While most of the parents understood how important Kirk was to our team at that time, we did have a couple that were jealous of Kirk and worried only about their own kids. Perhaps, this characterization was unfair, but it was how I saw it. I remember the varsity coach telling me not to worry about what a few people might say. For my part, I tried to take Kirk out as much as possible, but when I did our team would just fall apart. (I'm not bragging here, I am stating plain facts.)

As I've mentioned before, it wasn't as though Kirk was trying to steal all the glory from the other players. On the contrary, he always tried to involve his teammates. I think he made them better with his presence in the game. Kirk was an inspiring force on and off the court.

In this particular game we were four points ahead when one of the parents kept saying loud enough for me to hear, "He never takes Kirk out."

At that point, I decided I had heard enough. I sent someone in to take Kirk's place. When Kirk came off the floor he never complained. He just went down and sat on the bench. I went down to him and explained that I was proving a point and he understood. Less than a minute later we were seven points behind (an eleven point turnaround) and the team had not managed to get the ball over the ten second line. I got up, turned around, and looked at the man who'd spoken up earlier. I said, "Do you think it would be okay if I put Kirk back in now?"

He just dropped his head and wouldn't look at me. Kirk went back in and we won the game. I never had another problem with that man.

A COACH'S DREAM

Even when Kirk was young it was easy to see he was going to be an exceptional basketball player. He was one of those natural athletes and decided early that he wanted to concentrate mainly on one sport. The varsity coaches at North Vermillion all hovered over him. He was what a coach would refer to as a "coach's dream," like having another coach right out on the floor when he played. He had those certain qualities as a player you couldn't teach when he played. Kirk had a firm respect for his coaches and became close to them. They all loved him for his dedication to the game.

I think the respect and love they had for him probably became crystal clear at his funeral when every coach from throughout Kirk's life was there. Coach Brian Hughes came from southern Indiana, Coach Dave Hoffman from Lafayette, Coach Larry Hobbs from Muncie, Coach Mark Atherton from northern Illinois, and of course Coach Kirk Booe.

Coach Hobbs once told me that one of the big regrets he had at leaving North Vermillion was that he didn't get the opportunity to coach Kirk. Coach Atherton told me that after he resigned he thought he would never again come back to North Vermillion. This was the only thing that could have brought him back. He also said he came back because Kirk was a great kid.

I think Kirk received such attention from his coaches because he earned that special treatment through that intense commitment, his work ethic, and his love of the game. His coaches had no doubt that he respected them and he would always be there if they needed him.

SHORT CAREERS

Whenever Kirk came to stay with me he spent a lot of his time playing with kids in Catlin. So many of the fathers and coaches got to know him and knew what an excellent athlete he was. He ended up playing a couple of years of little league baseball in Catlin. But his short one year career of football also took place in Catlin. A couple of coaches asked me if I thought Kirk would want to play football so I asked him and he said yes. It was the first time he had ever played and he had a pretty good season.

One game in particular sticks out in my mind. Catlin was playing in Bismark, Illinois, and they had a rather large team. Kirk was playing defensive back and one of their big running backs got into the open. Kirk moved over to make the tackle and this running back just literally ran over Kirk. Kirk somehow got him down. Afterwards, Kirk just laid there so I went out on the field. When I got to him, Kirk looked up at me and said, "Man, dad that really hurt." Then I knew he was just shook up and he would be all right. Later when riding home from the game Kirk said, "Dad, is that what you call getting your bell rung?" I just smiled and said, "Kirk, that's just part of football."

Kirk did play football one more time but I don't know if I really count that. During his seventh grade year he played with the promise from the coaches that he would only play quarterback on offense. But when he saw my step-son Joe Brewer tear up his knee in practice he decided he'd had enough football. He didn't want to take a chance on getting hurt for basketball.

I really think had Kirk lived he might have played foot ball his junior year. Now we'll never know. All the kids and coaches had been trying to talk him in to playing. And just like in baseball I think he may have given it a try. I can remember one evening we were in the gym playing basketball and Coach Jim Puckett was standing beside me watching Kirk play ball. Kirk came down the floor and took the ball between his legs a couple of times, drove and pulled up and hit a jumper. Coach Puckett looked at me and said, "Are you sure you want him to play football?" And I said, "No, not really." But knowing his friends all wanted him to play, Kirk may have tried anyway.

* * *

Kirk's last two years of little league we moved him to Covington to play. He got to play more games and the competition was much better. Kirk played for a team called Lindees and had two really good coaches, Bruce Pierce and Clay Gerling. These two really worked with the kids and made it a lot of fun at the same time.

Kirk's second to last year they had tied for the league championship and lost in the tournament. The following season, Kirk's last one, everyone wanted to win it all. Bruce often told me how much he appreciated Kirk's willingness to work hard and how coachable he was. They played him everywhere—outfield, infield, pitcher, and sometimes even catcher. Kirk never complained. He just went where they told him. Kirk's team ended up winning the league championship and now it was time for the elusive tournament championship. During the game, it came down to the bottom of the eighth inning, two men on, two outs, and Kirk up to bat. A game only lasts six innings in little league so we had gone two extra innings. Kirk hit a three run homer to win the championship. It was a great way to end his little league career. He seemed to take it all in stride.

THE WHITE SCOOTER

When Kirk was in the fourth or fifth grade I took him to Danville to see about buying a motor scooter. Kirk wanted a way to ride around town. His brother and sister both had scooters when they were in junior high so naturally Kirk felt like he had to have one too. Of course, he got his earlier than they did. Dale and Deena had Honda Sprees and they would typically run up to 30mph. I planned to get Kirk his own spree since by that time the other two had been given to Kirk's cousins Brian and Kelli.

When we arrived at the store, Kirk's eyes lit up when he saw a white Yamaha Jog. It was more expensive than the Spree I had in mind but we ended up leaving with it anyway. The only thing is that I had no idea how fast this scooter could go until we had it home—it could run between 50 to 60mph. I nearly took it back but Kirk promised he would use it carefully. He kept it and rode it everywhere with a basketball strapped on the back.

Soon after, some of Kirk's friends got scooters too. He looked so funny riding that scooter; he was so small. When he would go down to my brother's house to stay a few weeks each summer he would bring his scooter along with him. Then he, Brian, and Kelli would travel around Rising Sun. Kirk absolutely loved that white scooter. It, like his basketball, became part of him. His was the only white scooter that zoomed around town, so if you saw it, you knew it was him. (After Kirk's death, his cousin Thad inherited the scooter.)

WHAT ARE REDNECKS?

Kirk had a friend on his AAU team named Maynard Lewis. Maynard was from Terre Haute South High School and later served as one of the pallbearers at Kirk's funeral. Maynard is a super basketball player and Kirk just loved being around him. Maybe the only difference between Maynard and Kirk was the fact that Kirk was white and Maynard was black. That didn't make any difference to Kirk. They both shared a love for basketball. Joey Bennett, Kirk's AAU coach, once said that when the AAU team went on the road he never had to worry about who roomed with whom. He knew Kirk would always be with Maynard, Tony Petty, and Frank Smith (the three black kids on the team). Not that it really mattered because all the kids on this team got along really well. But Joey always said that Kirk never saw color, only heart.

One time, when Maynard was home with Kirk for the weekend, Kirk and Maynard were riding around town on his scooter. He later came to me and said when they were riding through town some men out in front of the tavern had said some mean things to them about Maynard. I told him not to worry; they were just rednecks. Kirk asked me what their problem was and I tried to tell him. He said he didn't understand why people had to be that way. I told him that some people just weren't capable of understanding. I told him as long as he stood firm on his beliefs that was what mattered in the long run. I just told him to keep Maynard around the house or out at the gym so nothing bad would happen or no feelings would be hurt. I knew the more he played basketball the more black friends he would have and this would never make any difference to him.

WHO INSPIRED KIRK?

Being the athlete Kirk was I guess it was natural for his room to be cluttered with lots of sports memorabilia. It was what I referred to as a "sportsman's paradise." He had shelves in one corner filled with many trophies and awards he had won. (We donated many of these to the school to be put in his trophy case for the gym dedication. Now they're on display for everyone to see.) His walls were literally covered with pictures and posters and other sports materials. He had a chest with thousands of baseball cards, a safe with his more valuable cards, and we don't know what else. He was the only one who knew the combination and we didn't open it until a year after his death. He mainly collected Michael Jordan, Scottie Pippen and Damon Bailey in basketball and Frank Thomas, Ryne Sandberg, and Dave Justice in baseball. He had many valuable cards and starting lineup figures on his shelves too. Even though a lot of them were valuable, the sentimental value was much higher. He had so many knick-knacks from teams and a lot of Indiana University gear too. He spent a lot of time in his room watching television or reading.

Kirk received his first autograph sometime between the first and second grade. His mother and step-father had friends in Cayuga, the Coonces. Don Coonce was heavily involved in drag racing - even drove for Albert Clark at one time. While driving dragsters, Don became acquainted with Larry Nance, who was then a forward for the Cleveland Cavaliers, who happened to be a drag racing fan. In little time, Kirk was able to attend games with Don and he got to meet Larry Nance as well.

One day, Larry thought it would be nice if he sent Kirk an autographed picture of himself. Kirk enjoyed this immensely. Several weeks later, Don got a call at work from Nance who was laughing because that day he had received an autographed picture of Kirk. It was a school picture that Kirk had signed and sent to Larry because he thought it was the appropriate thing to do.

This was the first autograph Kirk had signed and I would remind him of it later when grade school kids would ask him for his autograph. He would always tease the kids and say, "Hold on to that. It may be worth something someday."

When my daughter Deena attended Indiana University Kirk would sometimes go down and stay with her. Every year he would learn where all the Indiana basketball players lived. He knew where they hung out, where they did laundry, what times they might be home. He hounded them for autographs or just a chance to talk to them. His passion was that someday he would wear an Indiana basketball uniform, maybe not be a star, but just be a part of the tradition. He loved going to the games at I.U. or watching them on television. He went to I.U. basketball camps. He thought players like Steve Alford and Damon Bailey were like God. He idolized them. He studied Steve Alford's tape and did his work out daily. I know he dreamed of someday being like them. Half his wardrobe of clothes was from I.U. Many of those autographs were buried with him.

As Kirk grew up he looked up to or tried to copy aspects of many players' games. But to me, he always had his own style, his own dreams, and he would never allow himself to be denied. While every father would like to be the one his son looks up to, I don't really know if Kirk ever truly looked up to me. We were always like best friends and we spent a lot of time together playing basketball. Kirk did ask a lot of questions about how it was when I played. He had read my scrapbooks about my game days and I know he wanted to do better.

My own claim to fame had been when I scored 39 points for a new North Vermillion scoring record during my senior year. He asked about this sometimes and wanted to know why I hadn't gone on to play basketball in college. I explained to him how I'd had a chance to play in college but instead I started my family at a young age and had no regrets about that. I have four wonderful children and wouldn't ever change that. I told Kirk what a golden opportunity he had and he could live the dream for both of us. I would help him do this.

At an early age I think like many other children Kirk wanted to "be like Mike." He was trying to be like Mike when he got his teeth caught in the net. He obviously looked up to Michael Jordan. He enjoyed the Chicago Bulls as a team in professional basketball and Indiana in college basketball. Like I mentioned before, Kirk collected Michael Jordan and Scottie Pippen basketball cards. I think he had 15 or 20 Scottie Pippen rookie cards. He looked up to Steve Alford because of his work ethic. He studied his tapes thoroughly. Calbert Chaney was also another favorite, but I think his very favorite was Damon Bailey. He even had pictures of Bailey on his basketball shoes. Kirk had role models of his own, but I don't think he ever realized what a role model he was for all the younger kids in our school. Even for adults. He was my role model, the only one I looked up to.

* * *

There was a movie about Pete Maravich called *Pistol*. Kirk must have watched this movie a hundred times. In fact, I think he lived this movie out every day of his life. I think the movie is about "Pistol" Pete's eighth grade school year. It shows him doing all of his fancy tricks with a basketball. Pete spent a lot of time just spinning a ball on his finger. Kirk would sit and do the same thing for hours. When we would go over to Cincinnati Kirk would sit in the van and spin a ball on his finger. He would eat or drink with a ball spinning on his finger. One of everyone's favorites was when Kirk would eat pudding with a ball spinning on the handle of the spoon.

One thing strange is that no one ever gave Kirk a nickname. He was always just Kirk. Not "Pistol" or anything else, just Kirk. If you heard the name Kirk you pretty well knew who they were talking about. I think if anyone who knew Kirk hears that name they will always think of my Kirk.

From the movie *Pistol,* Kirk also picked up other tricks. If they were hard to learn he would just work at them until he mastered them. Many times I would come home from work and Kirk would show me the new trick he had learned. He could spin the ball on every finger, take it behind his back, switch hands, and even bounce it off his head and into the basket. All the drills to increase your ability to handle a basketball he had mastered. The coaches always used him to display how to do a certain drill.

I remember when Kirk and I were at Lamar University in Texas. I was working at the camp and I always used Kirk to show how a certain drill was accomplished. He was the only in the seventh grade but I still used him to show even the high school kids. He would lie in his bed at night pretending to shoot a basketball to the ceiling just to work on his form. He would do this with or without a basketball. He worked so long and so hard at this that a basketball became like an extension of hand and arm. The best part about all of this was he could do all of this with both his right and his left hand equally.

I remember always teasing him about someday being a white Harlem Globetrotter. He used to tell me back that Coach Knight wouldn't allow him to do that at Indiana University. I imagine that Coach Knight would have adored him both as a player and a person. Why not? Everyone else did.

GIRLS? NOPE, BASKETBALL FIRST

Kirk never took a big interest in girls during high school. Sure, he had plenty of friends who were girls but he did not start dating anyone until just before he died. I remember a lot of teachers and some of Kirk's friends telling me that he could have had just about anyone he wanted. I don't know if that's true or not, but it really never mattered anyway. Kirk was not arrogant in any way, though some may have viewed him that way at different points. He simply wished to put all of his energy into basketball.

I remember many times when girls from other schools were calling the house for him, but Kirk wouldn't talk to them much because he had to play ball. He worried that too much talking would distract him from playing for too long.

When I brought up the subject of girls with him—a seldom occurrence—I would ask him questions. I would say, "Kirk, I think so and so is nice and cute too, don't you?"

Kirk would always answer 'yes' and quickly change the subject. He would also say that he wanted to play college ball first and then he would start thinking more seriously about girls.

I remember when he finally started dating. At first, it was a complete mystery to me—a closely held secret of sorts. I think when and if he wanted to talk about girls he would rather go and talk to Deena or Coach Zumwalt—never to Dad. At any rate, one night out at the school Coach Zumwalt came up to me in the coaches' office and asked if I knew Kirk had a girlfriend.

Of course, I said, "No way!" He said that Kirk mentioned it to him the previous night and said, "Man, Dad's going to kill me when he hears about this." Zumy told him he didn't think I would be mad. He said Kirk told him to tell me that his basketball play would come first.

To be honest with you, I was pretty happy for him. I think he needed some time away from the sport. After talking to Zumy, I went to find Kirk. I said, "Son, we need to talk." After finding out I wasn't upset we sat and talked more. While he and Brandy Howe only dated for a short time prior to his death, I think Kirk was able to experience the fun that is dating at least a little.

KIRK DANCING?

Early in Kirk's sophomore year he was voted to be the attendant for his class at homecoming—meaning he had to participate in all of the festivities during and after the game. He rode around the football field at halftime in a convertible with Meredith Darnell, who was the girl attendant for the class. After the game, he went to the dance and danced with Meredith during the king and queen's dance. I was the chaperone that night so I actually got to watch him dance. I think I was amazed that he knew how.

Sue Pence, who was one of Kirk's favorite teachers, was also a chaperone. Sue used to tell me that Kirk had this way about him that put you at ease. In her classroom, he just stepped in and practically took over—perhaps, you could say he was helping her. (Just as he did on the court, he would in the classroom.) She said that it was like he was the teacher. Everyone seemed to understand this but no one complained. I know she was devastated when she heard about Kirk's death.

The night of the dance several kids were asking Mrs. Pence to dance, but she told them she couldn't because it was inappropriate. Later I saw her dancing with Kirk. She came over to me smiling and saying, "I couldn't tell him no."

I remember that moment clearly. The Eric Clapton song *Wonderful Tonight* was playing while they were winding around the floor.

She told me that while they dancing, Kirk kept asking her, "Mrs. Pence, what's the name of this song?"

She replied, "You already know the name, Kirk."

Then he would say, "No, what is it?"

She gave up and said, "My you sure look wonderful tonight."

He'd say, "Thanks, you look pretty good yourself."

She told me she could have shot him.

After Kirk died, Sue brought me a recording of this song and reminded me of the story. She said that every time she heard that song she would think of Kirk and start crying. She also told me that her classroom was never the same after he was gone. No one could ever replace him.

VEGAS TRIP

One of my fondest memories and funniest times with Kirk was our trip to Las Vegas during the spring break of Kirk's freshman year. Included on this exciting journey were Dave Erwin, his son Grant (an eighth-grader), myself, Kirk, and my stepson Joe Brewer. We drove so we could see the sights along the way. We were gone for ten days. Some of the sights we saw were the Grand Canyon, Hoover Dam, the ski slopes in Vail, the Crater, the Painted Desert, and many others.

We ended up staying in Vegas for three days. We had rooms at Circus Circus and the kids had a blast playing the games in the Big Top. We did so much, but I want tell you what Kirk enjoyed the most. Our little group visited the Thomas Mack Arena, taking the opportunity to explore the inside. This was where the UNLV Rebels played basketball (Kirk was a fan of UNLV). A man came up to meet us and I told him I coached basketball at North Vermillion and I wanted to show the kids the arena. The man was very nice and took us on the grand tour.

Unfortunately, the ice was on the floor for ice hockey. Our guide gave us great seats for the hockey game and opened the gift shop so the kids could get souvenirs. He also gave the kids passes to go play ball at their practice facility. We left and ate at the Hard Rock Café. Afterwards, we took the kids back to play ball. They played for two hours and when Dave and I went back to pick them up Kirk was enamored by the fact that there were a couple of UNLV players there and he didn't want to leave.

I remember him telling me that this was the best part of the whole trip. I'm sure he enjoyed everything we did but that stood out for him.

I also recall stopping one day and renting a motel room for two hours to watch Indiana play Temple in the NCAA tournament. (Dave Erwin still tells me often how glad he was that we took that trip.)

IMPERSONATIONS AND MR. METZ

Probably one of the really funny things Kirk could do is impersonate people. I always thought whenever he did impressions he was still respectful. I don't believe Kirk was ever intentionally cruel or unkind. One of his best impersonations was of Mr. Metz, a teacher at North Vermillion.

Kirk respected Mr. Metz immensely. He used to tell me that many of the kids thought Metz was strange or peculiar but he said to me, "Dad, Mr. Metz can do everything well." He even got to the point where he would go bowling or golfing with Mr. Metz—sometimes he would get friends to tag along too. They always had a wonderful time. Kirk even made Metz's name out of wood in shop class. He kept on the headboard of his bed the rest of his life. Dale eventually gave it to Mr. Metz.

Metz told me that it was one of his most prized possessions. I'll never forget him taking Kirk's hand at the visitation saying, "Goodbye, my friend." They had a friendship based on a mutual respect.

Kirk had a few other great impersonations. He did a great Dave Erwin with his "gosh dog it" expression. Then there was Coach Atherton with his "North Vermillion pride," and Justin Tolley's dad, Greg. I'm sure he probably had one of me too when I wasn't around. Still, Metz was everyone's favorite.

DO I LOOK LIKE MY DAD?

About a month before Kirk died we were in the gym playing basketball. Probably around twenty or thirty people were playing. I was playing also that night but at this particular moment I was on the sidelines. Whenever I wasn't playing I was usually at the north end of the gym leaning with my back against the wall mat. Just a few feet down from me, Chris Moore and Geramie Million, who we called Nibs, were also leaning on the mat. They were seniors and had been teammates of Kirk's on the basketball team. Kirk came over and leaned beside me. I had my shirt off since I had been playing and Kirk had his shirt off too. Kirk looked down at Chris and Nibs and said, "Hey, Chris, Nibs, do I look like my dad?" They both kind of shrugged their shoulders.

Now Kirk had this way of sticking his stomach out to make it almost look like he had a basketball stuck in his stomach. Now, I was admittedly getting older and could no longer whip up on Kirk in basketball. Yet, what he did next totally caught me off guard. After Chris and Nibs shrugged Kirk stuck his stomach out and said, "Hey, Chris, Nibs, now do I look like my dad?" I thought they would die laughing. I had to laugh too as I punched Kirk in the arm. I think the whole gym laughed and rightfully so. This was Kirk at his best.

KIRK'S LIFE, MY STORIES

The stories included in this chapter are my stories, my favorite stories or, perhaps, my most memorable ones about Kirk. They've been used to shape a sketch of his life and times as seen through my eyes. It is the only perspective I can honestly share. I know that many people have different memories of Kirk, and I am glad they have them. They will enrich any reading of this portrait.

I think I've gotten a better idea about how my son was viewed by the many friends and acquaintances he had during his life. The countless ones I've talked to or received letters and cards from have helped me see more of my son than I would have otherwise. I am grateful for that too.

I am aware that there could be more written here, more stories to tell, but if I were to include them all, I would need many more pages.

CHAPTER TWO

Four Days Of Hell

"It was a day unlike any other day, just one that will never be forgotten because we lost one who was so close to us all. Yes, it was a freak accident; but like his family, I have come to accept this because I know that God surely must have needed a great point guard for his basketball team."

~ Jimmy Lee Beasley Sr.

April 8th started out like any other ordinary day. Our baseball team was playing in the Banks of the Wabash tournament at Riverton Parke High School near Mecca, Indiana. I went to across the street from my house to eat breakfast at what was then the Logan 105 restaurant. This was about 7 a.m. I ate with Don Corey, our head baseball couch, Kory Zumwalt, the other assistant, along with myself. Sitting across from us were Linda Webb Meyers, her husband Greg, and their daughter. After breakfast, we headed out to the high school to prepare for the upcoming game with Riverton Parke. I remember calling Kirk to have him bring me a check so I could pay for his new baseball jerseys that had recently arrived.

When he arrived at the school we started handing out our jerseys. I called Kirk's name several times because he was in the gymnasium shooting baskets. Of course, making the next basket was more important to him than picking up his baseball jerseys. While I've said before that he was fairly good baseball player Kirk had only agreed to play if we, the coaches, wouldn't keep him from any basketball commitments along the way. It was a simple arrangement.

When it was time to go, Kirk climbed aboard the bus wearing his headphones as usual, probably listening to *Jock Rock* or some Bon Jovi album. I think music helped him relax for the games. When we arrived at the field, the previous game between Rockville and Turkey Run was about half over. On the adjacent diamond, the North Vermillion girls' team was playing softball. Kirk's girlfriend, Brandy Howe, was playing in that game so we walked over to see how they were doing. After watching the team play for an inning we began to warm up for our game.

I remember walking over to Kirk to ask him what Coach Corey had said just before we had gotten off the bus. He had his hat on backwards and said, "Sorry dad," as he turned around, then he said his usual, "Chill out, dad," and burst out laughing.

Once Rockville scored a victory over Turkey Run, it was time for North Vermillion to face off against Riverton Parke. It was an intense game and we won it in the last inning with Kirk scoring the winning run.

Afterwards, I went up to Kirk. "Was that exciting?" I asked.

He said, "It was awesome, Dad, but not as awesome as playing basketball!"

Kirk had not played baseball since little league, and already, after only our second game, he was showing promise to be a "good one," as Coach Corey put it. He had a natural aptitude for athletics. He really could have picked up any sport and excelled in it.

In between games we had about a half an hour to rest, and I remember Kirk eating and taking it easy. We were heading into the championship game against Rockville. His mother and stepfather had been at the first game, but had to leave to take Kirk's sister and three-month-old niece, Darby, home. I think it was the only game of Kirk's athletic career they had ever missed. I must admit I was glad that Diana and Deena, his sister, missed this game. They were spared from the horrible events to come.

We were confident going into the game, especially since we had just beat Jason Murphy of Riverton Parke. Murphy was probably the top player in our conference and had already signed to play college baseball at Indiana State University.

Besides that, Rockville was one of the favorites to win our conference.

I remember during our turn at bat in the third inning Kirk came sliding into third base. I was the third base coach and called time out. Kirk stood up and brushed himself off and said, "Dad, I don't get dirty like this playing basketball." He also had a "strawberry" (a skinned spot) on his leg from the slide.

As he stood by me at third base, teammate Charlie Bookwalter yelled over at us, "Isn't that a pretty sight, father and son together in competition!" Little did I know that this would be the last time that I would ever talk to or stand beside my son.

When we went out onto the field, tragedy awaited Kirk. He took his position in left field, and with two outs and bases loaded, it happened. There is no logic to it, no reason for it, at least that we can or will ever understand. I know that I won't be able to comprehend it in this life. I kept asking myself, why Kirk? Also, why did it strike Kirk? I mean, there were eight other players on the field, there were hundreds of spectators, and there were girls playing a field away. There was a boy at bat with an aluminum bat in his hand, a catcher, and umpire with metal masks on. There were trees and a high foul pole. There were no answers.

The most reasonable answer I ever heard came from Kirk's grandmother, Ima Lee Gebbink. She believed that God had that lightning bolt directed specifically at Kirk. It would be quick, he would feel no pain, and it would be so eventful that no one would forget it for a long time. In this sense, Ima Lee provided a spiritual interpretation of the events, one that offered the hope for meaning in what seemed like a meaningless event. She believed that the tragedy would open a lot of eyes and many hearts would turn to God. So many reach out to the divine when the world seems spinning out of control and nothing makes sense.

I've come to believe that Kirk's death held deeper significance, that it was the will of God. Its impact was wide-reaching and powerful. Since Kirk's death, many, many people have gotten baptized and come to Christ. Those who turned to God were motivated by the belief that they would be where Kirk was when they died.

My son had such an effect on so many people. It boggles the mind. Kirk lived the sort of life and touched people in such a way that I think it makes sense why he was chosen to be taken on that day rather than someone else.

When the lightning struck, I was looking straight at him. I seldom took my eyes off Kirk when he was playing ball. I never saw the lightning; I just heard the big clap of thunder. I knew Kirk was hit because smoke and steam rolled off his body. He just went stiff and toppled over backwards, seemingly in slow motion. When the loud clap occurred, the home plate umpire immediately called the game. As the players ran off the field, I was running out to Kirk, yelling, "Oh my God! Kirk's been struck by lightning!"

Then people began to realize what had happened. I was the first one to him. I thought he was dead when I got to him. He was so purple and had a smoldering smell about him. His eyes were rolled back and his mouth was open. He was so stiff and lifeless. The field umpire began to give him mouth to mouth and Steve Dunham (one of our player's parents) began CPR.

I still clung to hope, but in the back of my mind I knew there was nothing anyone could do. He was in God's hands. I'll never forget that sight. I see it every hour I'm awake, I see it in my sleep. I sometimes wish I hadn't been there because of the horror of it all. At the same time, I'm glad that I was because I know my Kirk didn't suffer that day. He was taken very quickly without any pain. He was taken in a very special way by the hand of God. Perhaps, the Lord wanted me there to see it all, not only so I could be with Kirk, but also to make an impression on me to bring me closer to Him. It's become my testimony. I was a witness to what really happened that day.

Standing there over Kirk, I prayed to God to spare Kirk. I begged and pleaded, saying every prayer I knew. I cannot help thinking of all those people on the ball diamond. Kirk had just been struck by lightning and still there were people on the field. It seemed strange that no one seemed concerned about anyone else being struck. I know I was in deep shock. I remember Coach Zumwalt comforted me for a while, and then Donna Dunham, Debbie and Larry Wickens, and I don't know who else. There were so many caring people there on that day.

At one point, someone said they had a pulse, but the doctor said he didn't think they ever did. Later, someone suggested, and I don't remember who, that the pulse they might have had was God giving Kirk the choice to stay with him or to come back to earth, but Kirk decided to stay because heaven is that wonderful. If this was true, then heaven must be a really wonderful place because no one had a more fulfilling life than Kirk.

I remember thinking that it took forever for the ambulance to arrive. When they pulled up, my spirits lifted a little because I thought now that there were experienced professionals on the scene, they would have some means to revive him. A lifeline helicopter also had been called to take Kirk to Indianapolis. I remember a policeman tried to get me to ride in the car with him to the Vermillion County Hospital in Clinton, Indiana. I told him no and that I was riding in the ambulance with Kirk. When we arrived at the hospital they took Kirk into the emergency room to try to save him. I went into the chapel and prayed. I prayed with such intensity in those quiet, bleak moments. There was this part of me that stubbornly held onto to that sliver of hope that something could be done. Once again, Donna Dunham, Debbie Wickens, and also Debbie's little daughter Karen were with me. I remember little Karen holding my hand telling me that everything would be all right. Even today I still believe that God was listening to all our prayers, but he has a special purpose for Kirk.

Those who were in that chapel by my side through all of this, praying with me, and comforting me will always have a special place in my heart. I've never forgotten them. It is in times like these that one learns who their real friends are.

After what seemed like hours, but I'm sure were really minutes, the doctor on call came in to see me. He said he had tried everything he knew to try. He held out tiny thread of hope that perhaps the lifeline doctor on route from Indianapolis might know what else to try. He then told me that I needed to prepare myself for the worst. He thought Kirk was gone, something I had feared all along.

Shortly after the doctor left the chapel, Kirk's mother and stepfather arrived. I remember walking out of the chapel and looking at them saying, "Kirk's dead, he's gone."

Diana looked at me in shock and asked what happened? Pat, Kirk's step-father, beat the walls, and cried out, "Not Kirk, anybody but Kirk."

Then Deena arrived with her husband Junior to hear the awful news.

By then, the lifeline doctor had arrived from Indianapolis and came into the chapel to tell us that Kirk was definitely gone. All hope was lost. God had wanted him and had taken him. The doctors told us that they thought Kirk was probably dead the instant the lightning had struck him. One doctor said that Kirk's internal organs were so badly charred that organ donations were out of the question.

Before we left the hospital we were allowed to go in to see Kirk. It was like he was lying there asleep. He was such a handsome boy, so broad-shouldered and well built. He was just starting to change from a boy to being a young man. The mark on his forehead where the lightning had entered was no bigger than the tip of my little finger. Where it came out on the side of his foot was also no bigger. I still think that this was another way of God showing his love for Kirk. We would be able to show Kirk at the visitation and the funeral. Friends and family would be able to say goodbye to Kirk properly. As I said, it was almost like he was just laying there asleep. Leaving that room and saying goodbye that day was the hardest thing I ever did.

Away from the hospital, I realized that we needed to let friends and family know what had happened. I was so overwhelmed with grief and still in shock. I remember calling my brother, P.G., in Rising Sun, Indiana and telling him the horrible news. Both he and his wife Paula were so shook up they couldn't talk on the phone. Paula's mother got on the line and I asked her to call my sister in Atlanta, Georgia. We were trying to contact Dale, my oldest son, and Scott, Kirk's stepbrother. My two step-children, Joey and Jennifer, were waiting for me at home.

By that time, the news had spread quickly. I know there were reporters at the hospital. An outpouring of sympathy and support came flooding in from friends and relatives. It was a constant stream of people the rest of that evening and for some time after that. I remember that night I never slept a wink, nor the next night after that. I cried and cried. I never knew the human body could retain so many tears. I can't even imagine how many tears were shed for Kirk. I found myself wandering the streets of Cayuga all night long. I went to my friend Dave Erwin's house at four o'clock in the morning and they were still awake. Dave, his wife Barbara, and I all cried some more. None of us could understand why. Why did this happen to Kirk? In those early hours, I struggled to find any meaning in what transpired on that baseball field.

I wasn't there when the bus returned back to school the evening Kirk was killed. But, I've been told by many how awful it was. Upon hearing the news that Kirk was dead there were many, many broken hearts. Some sought solitude on our own baseball field while others went to the gymnasium. As many more kids and adults made their way to the school, counselors and preachers were sought out to help comfort all the students that were there. I know from talking to many teachers that the shock was still there even at the end of the school year.

* * *

In the days after Kirk's death, Diana took care of the arrangements and picked out Kirk's casket. I had only two requests. The first was to have his funeral in the North Vermillion High School gymnasium, the place that meant so much to him during his life. The second was that he be buried in his blue North Vermillion basketball uniform. It had the gold number four trimmed in white. Kirk had picked out this number himself when we ordered the new uniforms for this season. Also a basketball was placed in the casket along with the four awards Kirk had won in basketball at North Vermillion during his freshman and sophomore years. We knew we had to put a basketball in the casket with Kirk. He never went anywhere without his basketball.

We had all decided on the blue uniform for different reasons. One was that it was his favorite. Another reason was that we felt that he was going to be on the road with Jesus so his road uniform was the proper one to wear. Another reason was that there were already plans to retire his jersey in basketball and we thought the white home jersey would be the appropriate one to hang in the gymnasium. Kirk always told us that someday his jersey would be retired; we just never thought it would be like this.

We planned to have his visitation at the Cayuga Christian Church because we knew the funeral home would not accommodate all the people. Kirk popularity in the community demanded it. He had touched so many people, so we knew that we had to have a funeral that would accommodate everyone. I went over some of the numbers in my head, trying to estimate what we could expect. No one, not even the funeral directors, was sure how many would show up at the visitation and the funeral.

North Vermillion had about 300 students at the time. The town of Cayuga had a population of less than a 1,000 people while neighboring Eugene, where Kirk lived, had about 100 people. The North Vermillion gym held around 2,500 people. The family was supposed to arrive at the church an extra two hours early because of the expected turnout. We intended to be at the visitation from 3:00 to 9:00pm. This would not be nearly enough time.

THE VIEWING

I arrived at the church around 2:15 p.m. Inside the main doors there is a front hall that separates the entrance from the main sanctuary. A series of windows lines one side so you can see the sanctuary and the altar. I could see Kirk lying in the casket in the front of the altar. There were so many flowers. The altar was full of flowers. The aisles leading to the altar were full of flowers. In the back hallway, tables were set up and they were full of flowers. There were rows and rows of flowers. Later, I learned that there were more than four hundred bouquets of flowers. I'll never forget how overwhelming the fragrance was.

The family had thirty minutes to be with Kirk before the public arrived, but already at 2:30 some visitors were there. I remember we all just cried for the entire thirty minutes. The whole family, all of us were crying, crying hard, not wanting this to be true. Kirk was our life! We had supported him in everything he did. Not just Diana and I, the whole family supported him. He was so involved in everything. We had spent so many hours in so many gymnasiums watching him work so hard to attain his goals. Now it was all over. We even questioned ourselves, wondering if maybe he was taken because we were so wrapped up in him. But then we knew that couldn't be true. Ours is a loving God, a caring God. We were doing the right thing by being supportive of Kirk. God just had bigger and better plans.

At 3:00 p.m., the people started to filter in. At the entrance, by the registry, Diana and Deena had put together a photo album of Kirk that included pictures from his birth to the present. This gave people something to look at while they waited in line. Also the baseball cap he was wearing was on the table. It showed the tiny hole in the bill where the lightning had passed through. Other mementos of Kirk's life were also on the table. The line began to form.

P.G., Paula and their children Brian and Kelli had just arrived from Rising Sun, Indiana at about 2:30. My sister Betty and her daughters Michele and Deidre had also arrived from Atlanta, Georgia at about the same time. I was grateful to see them again and have their support. We had always been a close-knit family. Everyone followed Kirk and what he did. Deena said that even though Kirk was only sixteen, we all looked up to him. This was so true.

Later as the line grew longer it began to get colder outside. Someone said the line was three blocks long. At this time a maze was set up in the all purpose room in the church and the people were rerouted through this so they could get out of the weather. Still, the line worked its way outside. Friends told me that they waited in line for two to three hours to view Kirk's body. Looking back, I regret that I didn't have the time to talk to those who came through that line at the visitation. There were so many people. All I could do was thank them for coming and give them a quick hug.

We stood there by Kirk greeting people from 3:00 p.m. until after 11:00 p.m. We would have stood there all night if necessary. For a while I thought we might have to. Later many people told me that they had come to the visitation, but upon seeing the line, they knew they couldn't wait that long.

One thing that really amazed me was the variety of people at the visitation. There were many athletes from other schools, coaches, cheerleaders, friends, and many people we didn't even know. Every coach Kirk had ever had for any sport attended. They all spoke highly of him, saying what an inspiration he was not only to his teammates, but to them also as coaches. His little league baseball coach, Bruce Pierce, told me he still used Kirk as an example of how he wanted his players to be. He said he would continue to use him as an example. Bruce and his family placed a star of the game ribbon in Kirk's casket. He had won several of these when he played ball for Bruce. On the back of the ribbon where the date was to be written, they simply wrote "ALWAYS!" This was a tribute to Kirk for a positive impression he had made on someone.

I don't know how many people passed through and told me that Kirk was their best friend, both boys and girls. He was always kind to everyone. By so many saying that Kirk was their best friend, I think it was another tribute to Kirk for being so kind and caring to everyone, regardless of who they were or what they did. Skateboarders and thrashers came, showing that even though they had nothing in common with Kirk they still loved him and looked up to him just the same. One of them told me that Kirk was the only one they never teased for not doing bad things. They never tried to tempt him because they respected him and admired him for his kindness and his talents in athletics. They said they enjoyed watching him play too much to try to get him to be a part of their crowd. They said he was always nice to them. Some of them even told me Kirk was their best friend!

Many people tried to offer me sympathy and comfort by telling me they knew how I felt. Well, they didn't know how I felt! No one knew but me. My wife didn't know, my kids didn't know, Kirk's mom didn't know, no one knew—just me. Just like I don't know how they feel. The basic truth of the matter is that when we grieve, we ultimately do it alone. Each of us, in our own way, bears the burden of loss and deals with the pain. For anyone who has lost a loved one, I'm sure they may know something of the pain I felt or the loss I experienced. Kirk was my son, and I was his father, but we were also best friends too. I dedicated so much time to seeing him realize his potential. I shared in his victories as well as his failures. Ironically, I Kirk still plays a significant role in my life. Our relationship was special in many, many ways. I know my daughter had a special relationship with him also, as I'm sure his mother did too. I'm sure they probably thought of him as a best friend too. My daughter was the one he often confided in about certain things. I'm sure my sons Dale and Kaleb had their thoughts and feelings about Kirk too.

At one point, I remember standing by the casket. I reached in and felt under the white tee shirt he wore under his jersey. I was feeling for the cross I had given the funeral director to put around his neck. It was the cross my mother had given me when I was in grade school just before she had died. I had always told Kirk that when I died I wanted him to have it to wear around his neck. I had never dreamed that he would die before me. Now it was only fitting that he wore it forever. I had never touched a dead person before. He was so cold, so stiff and hard. I stood by the head of the casket and kept touching his hair, for that was what felt most natural to me. I was always afraid to touch a dead person, but not now. Kirk's death changed how I felt about many things.

We stood there by Kirk's casket for eight hours, never once leaving. Kirk's mother and stepfather, and I never sat down, never moved more than a few feet, greeting people as they filed, ever slowly, ever somberly, past Kirk. I wish I had a file of everything everyone said as they walked by. I wish I could have read all their minds to know what they were thinking about Kirk, what memories they were reliving. People left pictures, letters, and money they owed Kirk in his casket. Little kids left shirts they had worn with his number and name on the back. Teams left balls autographed by their players. Friends left mementos from school, necklaces, chains, and other items. Everyone cried as they walked by, some more than others. Some broke down and some tried to be strong, though most couldn't. Little kids told me how they had Kirk's autograph hanging on their wall. Everyone spoke of how unbelievable it was, how it was like their worst nightmare. The people in our area will always remember where they were at and what they were doing when they heard the news about Kirk.

The whole visitation reminded me of Kennedy's funeral procession or all of the fans that gathered when Elvis Presley died. I was genuinely shocked by the fact that Kirk was a hero to many more people than I had ever dreamed of. I'll never forget two girls from South Vermillion High School. Their names were Wendy and Brooke. They were there before the official start of the visitation at around 2:45, and they never left. They sat there on the front row the whole night. Every time I turned around, there they sat, every so often they would come up to pat me on the back or give me a hug, just something to show how much they cared.

I remember some of the best compliments I received on Kirk were from our rival coaches from other schools. They all said a lot of the same things. Some said when a kid has the talent Kirk had they are often braggarts or very egotistical. They all said Kirk was never like that. They all commented on how much they enjoyed sitting back and watching him play, even if he was on the other team. They loved talking to him and just being around him. Kirk was apt to talk about the strengths of the other players—even those of the other team. He never talked about himself. Opposing players also spoke highly of him, both as a person and an athlete. He had such a magnetic personality and was such a pleasure to be around, one couldn't help but like him.

Our preacher, Andy Spencer, said it was a testimony in itself about the kind of kid Kirk was that so many people attended the visitation that day and the funeral the next. He said it was also a testimony because so many people came to Christ as a result of the tragedy. I think if Kirk had been taken in a car wreck or some other way it would not have had the impact that this had. That's why he was taken by the hand of God, in a special way, to have this kind of impact!

At the same time, we also looked for little things too and gave thanks for them as well. Two of the pallbearers for Kirk's funeral had been enemies. They were always trying to pick fights with each other, yet they were both good friends of Kirk. One was an AAU basketball teammate of Kirk's from another school, while the other was a classmate of Kirk's at North Vermillion. (Now they are friends and talk about Kirk quite often.) Other students at North Vermillion told me that a lot of the petty jealousies at school had been forgotten mainly because all these kids had looked to each other for support to help them get through this tragedy. If Kirk had any enemies I didn't know about them. I really believe that he was a friend to all. He had that uncanny knack for always looking on the bright side of things.

I wanted to share another story from that day. During the visitation, a mother came to us and told us that her son had sent their bouquet of flowers himself. These people had little money and their son was not very popular. In fact, he was the kind others always made fun of. She also told us that Kirk was her son's best friend. She said Kirk was the only boy who didn't make fun of her son. She said it would make her son's day whenever he would see Kirk and Kirk would say hi to him. This boy was in special education, but it didn't make any difference to Kirk.

* * *

At about 8:00 on the night of the visitation Kirk's little brother Kaleb returned from Florida. He had just turned eight years old three days before Kirk's death. Kaleb had left the morning of Kirk's death to fly down to Florida for spring break. I had to call him that night and tell him his big brother had been struck by lightning. Kaleb flew back home Monday morning. It was the quickest flight he could get back to Indianapolis. Also Seth Dunlap, one of Kirk's pallbearers, was in Florida on spring break. Seth was an AAU teammate of Kirk's and was a sophomore at Terre Haute South High School. Seth and his mother flew home on Tuesday morning for the funeral. Traveling all this way was another way of showing love and affection that was felt for Kirk.

Even though Kirk teased him constantly, Kaleb thought the sun rose and set on Kirk. He loved him and looked up him. Kaleb had a hard time truly understanding what had happened to Kirk. He kept asking if Kirk was coming back. After a while—I'm talking weeks—he realized that Kirk wasn't coming back. Like so many others, he just broke down. It happened at the cemetery one day. He ran back to the van to the back seat and started crying. I told him that it was okay to cry up here, that everyone does that. When we got home he went straight to his room and wouldn't come out for hours. Kaleb emulated his older brother. He asked for Kirk's number thirteen in baseball. He wore Kirk's glove when he played, even though it was nearly as big as he was. When he played basketball he asked for Kirk's number four and constantly asked if he was doing something how Kirk did it. Kirk was very much alive in his heart and in his mind.

People came through the line at the visitation, commenting that we were holding up well. I think there comes a time when you've cried so much that you can't cry anymore. After standing there for hours I had become numb as to what was going on. Again, people don't see you when you're alone to think about things. I was amazed at how strong Kirk's mother was through all of this. But, I also know that she had her hard times too. I look back on all this now and wonder how we ever made it through without falling apart. I know I didn't eat or sleep for days. I'm sure Diana and Kirk's other relatives and friends didn't either. I found myself trying to comfort everyone else. There were so many children hurting so badly. I kept telling all the little kids how much Kirk loved them and how much he talked about them.

Close to 9:00 p.m. the funeral director came up to us to see if we wanted to cut the line off. We said no. We would have stayed there all night anyway. As it was, after the visitation ended at eleven o'clock, many people came to the house just to talk. We spent the whole night just telling our favorite Kirk stories.

* * *

There a couple of stories I wanted to mention before we continue. They involve my son Dale and my brother P.G.

When Dale went to Danville, Illinois to buy a new suit for Kirk's funeral the tailor told him he would try to have the suit ready by Tuesday but he doubted very much if it would be. When Dale wrote the check out for the suit the man noticed his last name was Gentrup and asked Dale if he was related to Kirk. Dale told him that Kirk was his brother. Dale asked the man if he knew Kirk. The man said no, but he had read a lot about him the newspaper. The man told Dale if he would wait they would alter his suit right then and there. Dale walked out with that suit the same day.

My brother P.G. had chosen to stay in a motel in Danville, as did my sister Betty and their families. When they were checking out and paying the bill, P.G. noticed that the bill was much cheaper than he had been quoted. He brought the mistake to their attention. He was told that they knew why he was in town and they wanted to show that they cared also. None of these people knew Kirk personally, but they had read about him in the papers or saw it on television. Both parties complimented my son and my brother on what a wonderful boy he must have been. They said they had heard so many people talking about Kirk the last few days that they felt like they knew him too.

LAYING HIM TO REST

The day of the funeral was not a day I was looking forward to. I knew it would be the last time I would ever see Kirk, at least in this life. The newspapers and television reporters had called and asked if they could attend Kirk's funeral. I told them if they were respectful they could attend. The funeral director told me he was worried about parking and seating everyone at the funeral. They hired extra help and had the police there to help direct traffic. North Vermillion High School sits on State Highway 63 and is a much traveled road. Later on, I realized they would indeed need the extra help.

When I walked into the hallway outside of the gymnasium I saw many familiar faces standing around. The first person I saw was my supervisor from work, Janice Reardon. She came over and gave me a hug and said how very sorry she was. I knew that many of these friends and relatives saw me as they would never see me again. Many others were waiting outside the gym because the family was to be the first to enter to see Kirk. When I walked into the gymnasium I saw they had Kirk's casket sitting at one of the free throw lines. It was an appropriate place because Kirk had spent so much time there shooting free throws.

I thought back to the times when Kirk and I were at that very same free throw line. Kirk would said, "Dad, let's have a contest. Whoever makes the most in a row, the other has to buy a pop."

We did this every time we went to the gym, but this one particular day I thought I had him beat. I stepped up to the line and proceeded to make twenty-eight in a row. I felt pretty safe with that number and I began to razz him about finally having to buy me a pop for a change. Kirk then stepped up to the line and made forty in a row.

Then he looked at me with that smirk of a smile of his, laughed, and said, "You buy."

We always shot until we missed and I remember this particular day Kirk missed on purpose because he knew I was aggravated. Kirk was always a good free throw shooter and we were competitive in this way. As a freshman he had a string of twenty-one straight over a few games, so I knew pretty well that I wouldn't beat him.

That gym was the only place I seriously considered to hold Kirk's funeral. It was his home away from home. He spend so much time on that court, many of them he spent by himself. I know there has never been anyone at our school who had the sort of dedication that Kirk showed every time he entered that gym. A lot of people, including myself, called him a "gym rat."

The gymnasium was opened an hour before the service so that more people could pay their last respects. More things were put in the casket: pictures, letters, balls, chains, necklaces, etc. His casket became like a time capsule. His body was nearly covered. Later the funeral director asked what we wanted left in the casket. We told him we wanted everything left in and he told us that he didn't know if it would all fit and still allow them to close the casket. He later told us that everything was left inside but some things had to be put down by Kirk's feet in order to fit everything inside. The outpouring of love and affection was just tremendous! I'll always be appreciative for the outstanding job that the Deverter Funeral Home did in handling Kirk's funeral. I know it was no easy task.

We had to pick eight pallbearers to carry Kirk's casket. I said it would have been easier to have picked a hundred. We chose Maynard Lewis and Seth Dunlap from Terre Haute South High School. They were both AAU teammates of Kirk's. Michael Crossley from South Vermillion High School, also an AAU teammate, was chosen. Maynard was a freshman, while Seth and Michael were sophomores. From North Vermillion High School, we had Grant Erwin, a friend and future ball player. Others included Justin Tolley, a senior, another teammate, and Jimmy Strubberg, a junior, a neighbor and good friend of Kirk's, and Jesse Wickens, a senior and another teammate. The last one was Doug Hollingsworth, another of Kirk's classmates and friends. Justin, Jesse, Kirk, and another boy named Courtney Hawkins would take turns staying at each others' houses on Friday nights. They all became good friends hanging out together. Kirk had pinned the name "The Posse" on them. The pallbearers all sat in chairs up next to Kirk's casket.

Only a few bouquets of flowers had been taken to the school. Others were taken to the cemetery while all the planters had been left at the church to be passed out later to Kirk's family and friends. The line that formed before the service wasn't very long because the gymnasium was opened only an hour before the service, but it became steadily longer. Deena spoke first at the service, then me. Then a letter was read from Pat Crowder, Kirk's step-father. A poem was read for Kirk's mother. A poem was also read that was written by Donna Dunham. It was the most fitting poem for the occasion. Since then, we have used it for other purposes. It has fast become my favorite piece of literature. Then our preacher, Andy Spencer, spoke. He gave a very warm and uplifting message and tried to help everyone understand why this all happened. I know it was a very difficult thing to try to explain.

Then the Bette Midler song *Wind Beneath My Wings* was sung by Brian Byrum, who was then the youth minister. There weren't many dry eyes in the gymnasium during this song. It ended up becoming my favorite song. Honestly, I don't think I'll ever be able to hear this song without thinking of Kirk.

Knowing that it was going to take a long time for everyone to pay their final respects to Kirk, we arranged for some of Kirk's favorite songs to play. We thought this might ease the tension a bit, and we also thought this was what Kirk would have wanted us to do. We hoped we wouldn't offend anyone. I must admit it was different for a funeral. Even with the crowds moving through at a quick pace, it still took over two hours. I know saying that final goodbye to Kirk was hard on everyone.

Once everyone had left the gym, only the family was there again. As each family member made their way up to say goodbye to Kirk, I sat there thinking about how he was so important to all of us, how much joy he brought into all of our lives. If there is just one thing I can say Kirk, I would tell that he was always there for us. There was always enough of him to go around. I thought of all the fun times we had, all the serious times as well as the silliest. This would be my last memory of Kirk, the most lasting memory I would have of him. Thank God for memories, especially the good ones. I wondered what I would do without my Kirk.

After all the family had passed through, only Kirk's mother and I remained. We talked about what a wonderful child we had brought into this world. He had never given us any trouble. He had never brought us any sorrow, only joy and happiness. We talked of how he was a good student. He loved all of his teachers. His coaches reminded us all the time that he was a coach's dream, both because of his incredible athletic abilities as well as his dedication. Diana and I spoke of the day he was baptized. With the other things we learned about his faith, we felt sure that he was at peace in heaven. Then I left Diana to be with Kirk by herself for a few more minutes. I don't know what was said. It was a final intimate moment between a mother and her child.

When I left the gymnasium the Channel 10 News was waiting outside and asked if they could speak to me. I obliged and spoke of how Kirk was playing basketball for God now. They asked if I minded if they filmed some things. Once again, I said they could as long as they were courteous. I didn't know they were going to try and film Kirk's casket being brought out of the gymnasium. My oldest son Dale jumped out of his car and told them they weren't going to film his brother's casket. This bothered him, and I understood. At that time, I realized that he was a man himself now. Dale was thinking more clearly than I was on that day. I was very proud of him at that moment. The news people moved on down and interviewed some people and filmed the processional leaving the school. I think all my children did a lot of growing up during those four days. I also think that perhaps at the same time, I did a lot of aging.

* * *

As the processional made the way up Highway 63, I was reminded once more of the day that Kirk died. As we made our way out of Riverton

Parke baseball field in the ambulance, there were people standing along the way applauding Kirk and yelling for him to pull through. Many people were crying and clinging to each other for support. I remember one elderly lady standing and praying and another with her fist in the air as if to tell him to keep fighting and to be strong. The same was true the day of the funeral. People were parked along the highway waving and applauding and showing more support for Kirk. The police were directing traffic out of the school parking lot, and I was later told by someone stopped in the traffic that they waited for almost twenty minutes.

The eight-mile trip to the cemetery seemed like an eternity. As we drove up the hill and turned to enter the cemetery I looked back and could see the line of cars stretched as far as I could see. I was later told that the cars were still coming out of the school as we were turning into the cemetery. Dale told me of three large signs erected on some tall trees in some yards along the way. One said: We Love You Kirk. Another said: We'll Miss You. The third said: You're the greatest.

Once we arrived at the cemetery the funeral director told us to remain in the car because it was starting to drizzle. He said it would take at least a half an hour to park the cars. I sat there thinking back again to when Kirk and I were visiting the grade school. Little kids would come up to him and ask him for his autograph. He would always be kind of embarrassed by this but he would always sign. These same kids now would always cherish these autographs from Kirk.

He always told us that someday he would be giving autographs and he would be a good role model for kids. As I sat there waiting for all the cars to park, I realized what a good role model he was, not only for kids but adults as well.

After the cars were parked we made our way over to the tent at Kirk's gravesite. Gathered around the plot I looked at another grave. Kirk was going to be buried by his Uncle Donnie, someone he had never known. Donnie was Diana's brother. He had died at the start of his freshman year of high school. His was also an unusual death. The similarities between Kirk and Donnie were sometimes eerie. A lot of Kirk's family believed that Kirk reminded them of Donnie. A friend of Donnie's even wrote that at Kirk's visitation he saw Donnie in the casket and not Kirk. This person wrote that Kirk had reminded him of Donnie when he played basketball and even thought he looked a lot like Donnie. Donnie also had been a good basketball player, a good Christian, and a good role model for many. Kirk's grandparents, Donnie's parents, had commented that Kirk's life had almost been like God letting them relive Donnie's life all over again. Then, once again, at such a young age, he was taken. It was strange at times listening to them talk. We as a family feel that today Kirk and Donnie are together in heaven, maybe even that Donnie was the one to meet Kirk at the gates of heaven to lead him into the Kingdom of God.

Donnie had also died under unusual circumstances. He had an accident on his bicycle and had been taken to the hospital and was released, only to die the next day. Nobody understood why it happened, it just did, and everyone had to accept it. I had moved to Cayuga just before the start of my senior year. Diana's mom and dad had once told me that it was like I had been put here in Donnie's place. I became so much a part of their family. I even sat in Donnie's chair at graduation. (Since my last name was Gentrup, his being Gebbink put me in his exact seat.)

His parents spoke of how I took his spot on the basketball team and other school activities. It seemed to them that I was always there where Donnie should have been. Later, when Kirk was two years old, Diana and I were divorced, and her parents began to draw comparisons between Kirk and Donnie.

I mused on such things during the graveside service and it all seemed to go so fast. In no time, we were leaving Kirk there.

* * *

Afterwards, there was so much food sent to our houses that we decided to deliver some of it to needy people around the area. We sent food wherever we thought it would be eaten. I remember going to the post office for days after the funeral and they would have cards for us bound by rubber bands. There were so many cards. I knew there would be no way to thank everyone personally. The outpouring of sympathy and love was overwhelming.

* * *

I remember talking to a friend of mine, Larry Colson, after Kirk's death. Larry was an electrician and understood some of the mechanics of lightning, electricity, and conduction. He told me that he had been over to Riverton Parke High School and walked around, trying to figure out how that happened to Kirk. He said that if he didn't know any better he would say there was no way that happened at all. There were trees, flagpoles, metal fences, and so many other sources that should have attracted the lightning first. He couldn't figure out how it happened. I think that is part of the reason I called it an act of God. As I reflect on the events of those four days of hell, I will always feel that Kirk was handpicked by God.

Interior of the Cayuga Christian Church. Kirks' visitation.

CHAPTER THREE

Some Last Words

"I know several of you witnessed Kirk's death, but more of you witnessed his life. That's what's important."
~Diana Crowder, Kirk's mother

The events of those four days were mind-boggling and challenging beyond anything I have endured before or since. Even today it is difficult to express what was going on in my head then, though I have done my best to do just that. I am glad I did for it has given me a unique opportunity to share Kirk's story with you. Part of that story was the final words I said about him at his funeral.

Standing there in front of that crowd of mourning friends and loved ones, I delivered a message that I had prepared beforehand. I wanted to make sure I said everything I needed to say about Kirk. Such words were merely an encapsulation of a rich life, just a small measure of not only who he was but how I felt about him.

Rather than going on about what I wrote, let me share it with you. It appears as I wrote it and said it there in the North Vermillion gymnasium in 1995.

KIRK'S EULOGY

> Kirk Gentrup! How many times have you heard that name in this gymnasium? How many miles has my boy ran up and down this court? While some called him a gym rat, I called him a hard working, totally dedicated basketball player, always setting his goals high and always working hard to achieve them. To me this gym will always be Kirk's home away from home. This will always be Kirk's gym.
>
> Even though Kirk will always be remembered for his basketball first, he was so much more than that. He was a Christian first; he always took his Bible to basketball camp with him. He was totally dedicated to his family, just as his family was totally dedicated to him.
>
> As a father I was like any other father. My boy was special. I was sel-

fish. He was always "My Kirk." But, I always knew he wasn't just "My Kirk." He was Diana's Kirk, Deena's Kirk, Dale's Kirk, Kaleb's Kirk, Pat's Kirk, Scott, Jennifer, and Joe's Kirk, and I could go on. To us as a family, he was "Our Kirk." And now as I look out here today I know he was very much "Your Kirk." He gave us so much joy and happiness with his basketball talent, with his smile and laughter, and with his friendship. So yes, he was special. He was one in a million!

Kirk touched so many people during his 16 years with us. From the time he started to play biddy ball at the Y.M.C.A. to his last baseball game against Rockville, he touched so many lives. On the court he was always very competitive; he always wanted to win. But off the court he loved everyone, even his opponents. He was always the first to compliment the other team or the other player for an outstanding play. I can still hear him say, "Man dad, that was bad, just awesome!"

Kirk always told his mother and I we would never have to pay for his college education, that he would do it himself by playing basketball. He always said, "Dad, I'm going to play on the next level." When he died I thought he'll never get to accomplish this goal, he won't get to play on the next level. But now I firmly believe that he is playing on the next level. In fact he's playing on the highest level. He is now the best point guard in heaven!

I'm not going to mention individual games or exploits on the basketball court by Kirk. I want everyone to remember their own special play or game. Sunday night I sat with Geramie Million, Chris Moore, Zach Dunham, and Charlie Bookwalter and we talked about Kirk's life and realized then just how many people he did touch and how everyone has their own special memories.

I really can't mention all the names because there are so many, but Kirk was especially proud of his AAU basketball team and the things they accomplished. I want to thank Joey

Bennet and Chris Barrett for the competition and travel he enjoyed. I want to thank his coaches and teachers who all meant so much to him. We all know that teachers have pets and I'm here to tell everyone that Mrs. Dreher did have a pet and it was Kirk. Mrs. Pence, I think Kirk thought the world of you, he talked of you so often. Mr. Metz, I'll never forget Kirk mocking you in class. This was his way of showing how much he admired you. Mr. Erwin, Coach Booe, Coach Corey, and Coach Zumwalt, we all know how you felt about him and how he felt about you.

We as a family all feel Kirk was taken for a reason. You know Kirk had a girlfriend, finally! Her name is Brandy. But he also had a very special little girlfriend. He so loved his little niece Darby that we feel he is now her special Guardian Angel. He'll now be with her everywhere she goes. When he went home and told his mother he had made the baseball team he said he would play left field because he had "wheels." (By saying he had wheels he meant

> that he was fast afoot.) We feel that those wheels have been turned into wings and he is now a Guardian Angel for God.
>
> In closing I want everyone to remember Kirk. Keep him in your thoughts. Keep him in your prayers. I want to thank everyone for helping us through our time of grief. Once again, it's not fair to say names but you all were so kind and caring. Your friendship was so precious to us all. Kirk was special; don't ever let him leave your hearts, don't ever let him leave your minds. Remember always: As a father he is "My Kirk." As a family he is "Our Kirk." As friends he is "Your Kirk." Thank you all very much for everything, we love you all!

They were such public words, written for that particular audience. They were just a brief summary. There were more words I wanted to say but they were not all right for that moment. I knew that I had to write Kirk a letter to say goodbye and tell him how I felt now that he was gone. So, I did. Here is the letter that I wrote. It was written at a time when the pain was sharp and clear, when the sense of loss was incredible. My heart was heavy and my spirit was crushed.

A GOODBYE LETTER

Dear Kirk,

Saying goodbye to you is the hardest thing I'll ever have to do. I don't even have to try to imagine anything being harder because I know it's not possible. Losing my own parents at such a young age was hard but it doesn't even compare to the pain of losing you. One thing I hope and pray is that now maybe you know your grandparents, my mom and dad. I know they would have been so proud of you, as we all were so proud of you.

I know I still have Dale, Deena, and Kaleb here with me, but it's just not the same without you. And it's not that I loved you any more than them. I guess maybe it's because they're still here and you're not. I think we all had a mutual love for each other but you know how we all followed you and what you did. We were like your shadow.

Dale pretty much keeps his feelings to himself, I never really know what he's thinking or feeling. I think he'll handle it better as time goes on. Deena on the other hand doesn't handle it well at all. She's a lot like me. She doesn't want your memory to ever die. It doesn't take much to set her off. I thank God for Darby. Otherwise, I think Deena would not have gotten through losing you. As for Kaleb, he's young and I know he thinks about you a lot by what he says. But, I don't think he really totally understands. All he knows is that you're gone and he's never going to see you again. I know that has to hurt a lot.

As for me, well words are not ever going to explain how I feel. I feel a hurt I'll never feel again. I feel a pain that I can't do anything to cure. I feel an emptiness that I can't do anything about. I live, but it's not much of a life. I lost a child, a son, a best friend when I lost you. Kirk, I really think, I really feel the happiest day of my life will now be when I die and get to be with you again. I know I have some purpose on this earth and I'll live until that purpose is served but my true happiness will be seeing you again someday. I know that maybe I need to be here for Dale, Deena, and Kaleb, and I so enjoy Darby, but it doesn't take the place of your loss.

I think about you the first thing every morning when I wake up. I think about you the last thing every night before I go to sleep. And I think about you all day long. I think I'll always do this. You were my pride and joy. You were my happiness, my dreams, and my ego. You were my life! In my heart and in my mind you'll never ever die. You'll always be a part of me.

People often tell me they don't know how I made it through all of this. They don't really know the truth. I didn't really make it through. I know I'm only a shell of what I used to be. When you died Kirk, I died right along with you. This life no long matters to me anymore. I only exist because it's God's will. My kids and granddaughter mean the world to me but even they can't fill the void of losing you. They are now my purpose on earth and that's the only thing that keeps me going.

In closing Kirk, I want to tell you that as a son you were the greatest. You were truly a gift from God. There's nothing I would have changed about you. Your looks, your personality, your smile, your dedication, your sense of humor, I would keep them all the same. When I say you were one in a million, I truly mean it! Diana and I were truly blessed to have had you. The fact that we had you for only sixteen years really doesn't matter. It was such a special and wonderful sixteen years and that's what really counts. We all have a lifetime of memories because of you.

I will see you again someday Kirk. Until then I love you and I miss you!

Love, Dad

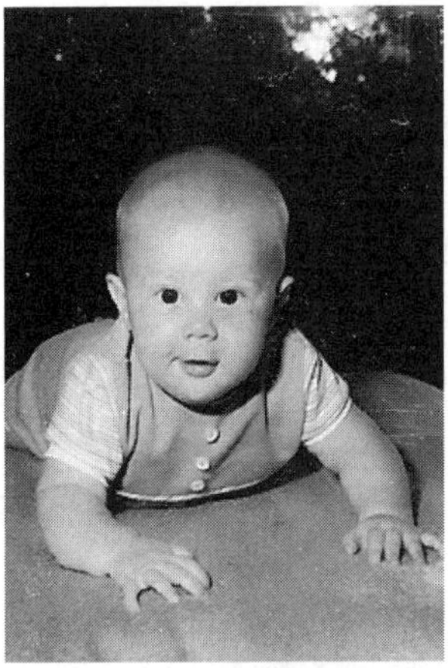

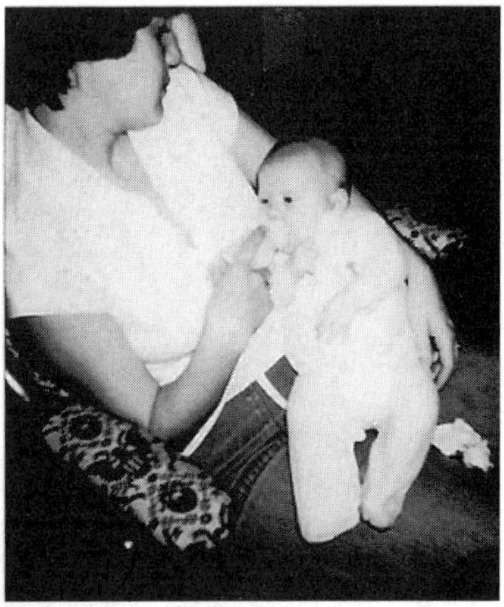

Top left: baby Kirk; top right: Diana and Kirk; middle left: Kirk's first day of school at Cayuga Elementary; middle right: Kirk outside the ball diamond; bottom left: Kirk in his football uniform

Kirk dunking the ball

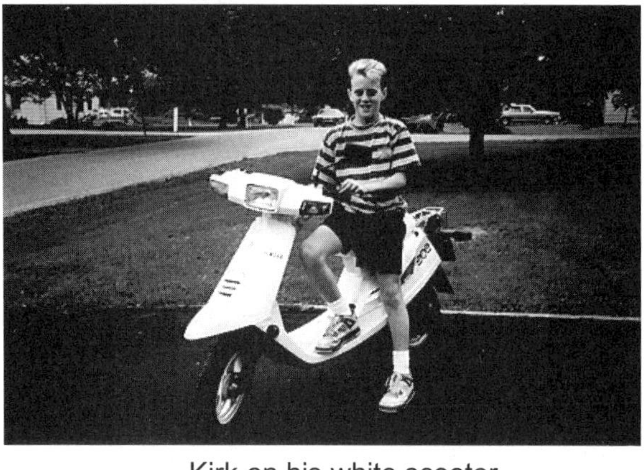

Kirk on his white scooter

Kirk and Don Corey in the Cayuga Elementary gym

Kirk playing in the pool with Winston

Kirk with Meredith Darnell

Kirk with "Mother"

Left to right: Grant Erwin, Kirk Gentrup, Joe Brewer, and Ken "Cruiser" Gentrup

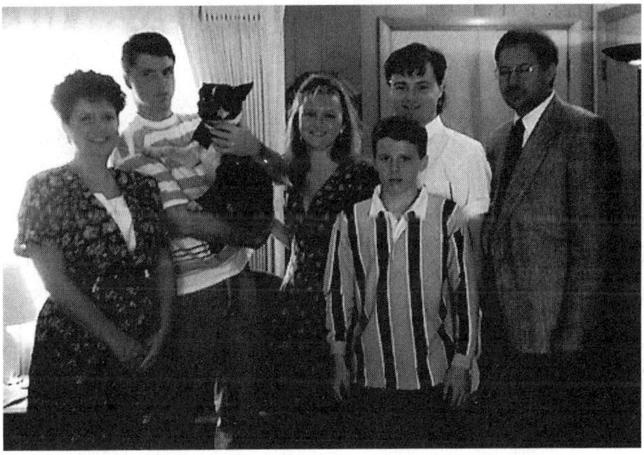

Diana Crowder, Scott Crowder, Deena (Gentrup) Martin, Kirk, Dale Gentrup, and Pat Crowder

CHAPTER FOUR

A Legacy In Letters

"Of all the people I feel badly for after Kirk's tragic death last Saturday, the most sympathy goes to the ones who never got to know him. Besides his athletic ability, he was a dream to be around and he brightened every room he entered.

~ Joey Bennett,
Tribune Star reporter and Kirk's AAU Coach

Many of the most potent reminders of the impact that Kirk's life had on others can be found in the number of people who came to his visitation and funeral. As I've already written about previously, hundreds of people turned out to pay their respects to my son. This was not the end of such expressions. Many others shared their thoughts and memories of Kirk in person, through letters, cards, and stories. Even today, people tell me what they remember about Kirk, those terrible days in April, and other stories. I still cannot believe the enormous volume of mail my family received in the aftermath of Kirk's death. I dare not try to make even a rough estimate.

In this chapter, I wanted to include a selection of the letters, notes, and other writings that reveal some of the reasons why my son was so loved and respected. It includes messages from classmates, friends, family, even complete strangers. Some were written to me; others were written for other purposes and later given to me. I have included names when I could to give credit where credit is due, but some pieces have come to me anonymously. I've collected so many pieces over the years. There have even been some that were found at the cemetery among the decorations on Kirk's headstone. They offer different glimpses of my son. I am grateful for them.

NOTES FROM KIRK'S FRIENDS

Mrs. Pence:

> I have so many fond memories of Kirk that it's really difficult to single out only one. I will always remember how Kirk could win me over with his beautiful smile. Regardless of how badly my day was going, when Kirk would walk into my room, or pass me in the hall, he would smile and say, "Hi! Mrs. Pence," I would then immediately

feel better. I miss him terribly, but I thank God I was fortunate enough to know and love Kirk.

Brandy Hughes:

One of my fondest memories of Kirk was when we were little kids and we used to go swimming in the pool and his dog Winston would jump in and swim with us.

Also, when Kirk, Chrissie, and I would go to Aunt Ruthie's after school and play Niagara Falls with his Hot Wheels and make fun of Chrissie because she couldn't ride a bike, even though she was older than both of us. He was a great cousin!

Brian Delp:

My favorite memory of Kirk is...well there are too many memories of Kirk. The memory I remember the most is when Kirk and I had Drafting class together. We would always think about what we would do to make the basketball team better.

Another memory is when we won the eighth grade WRC tournament. We worked together to win the trophy. Without Kirk's presence I wouldn't be the man I am.

Josh Baldwin:

I saw a smile every time I saw him.

Meredith Darnell:

I remember Kirk always telling me his future plans: To go to I.U., play on the team, and become a coach. He then would move into a huge mansion—where he said I could live with him—in the *servant's quarters!*

I always told Kirk he had it wrong and he would be my butler. And he would always say, "Why would I answer doors in my own house?"

Tiffanie Dunavan:

My fondest memories of Kirk would be when we were in grade school. In third grade we both had Ms. Jones and four our Christmas party Ms. Jones had the guys draw a girl's name and vice versa. I really liked Kirk a lot. I had no idea who had my name and I was really surprised when he handed me a present.

In second grade we were in the same group to go to Billie Creek Village. A mom (grandma) was the chaperone and we had a lot of fun. When we were on the hay ride we were the only ones that didn't get wet.

I remember in junior high and high school that even though we didn't have a lot of classes together he still talked to me. I remember how he was really popular and even though he was popular, he didn't let it go to his head. He didn't start thinking that he was better than anyone else. He didn't just talk to *his* kind of people. He talked to everyone. I loved Kirk and I miss him very much. I think about him every day.

Joel Wesch:

My fondest Kirk memory was the time that he and Joey came to my house, and we took the golf cart for a ride. We ended up in the middle of a recently plowed field with a dead battery. Needless to say, my father wasn't too happy with us, and I blamed it all on Kirk, even though it was all my idea.

Cindy Lewis:

I have many memories of Kirk. Some of the best were in our seventh grade English class where he autographed everything I owned. I will always remember him intercepting notes from me to Meredith, writing silly things on them, and his poems about cats and space ants. Kirk was a wonderful person with a great sense of humor. I will never forget him.

Katie Hicks:

My fondest memory of Kirk is how he always walked by me and said, "Hey Cath," which we suppose is short for Catherine, my real name. It always made me smile because no one else ever called me that, even to this day. Sometimes that's what I miss the most. Just his day to day hellos.

Another great memory of mine is of course about basketball. When we were little kids we used to play at Joel's house in the basement. He always beat us and if we won it was only because he let us or he must have been sick which even then he killed us. It's funny how we used to get mad and always tease him that he must have cheated, but we knew he hadn't, he was just good. These are just two of the many memories of Kirk that I have and I will cherish them always.

Grant Erwin:

My fondest memory of Kirk is when we would ride our mopeds to Gessie and play ball and make fun of the Hollowells.

Nick Stambaugh:

Playing basketball in Gessie beating us senseless. Schooling us left then right-handed. Trying to play defense when it was like playing in cement shoes.

Joe Congleton:

My fondest memory of Kirk was during basketball camp. He often complimented me and helped me out when the other kids yelled at me for making mistakes.

Amber Pasquale:

When Grant, Jimmy, Kirk, and I were going to a football game in Junior's old Tracker with the radio full blast.

When Kirk taught me how to dribble a basketball behind my back at Jimmy's house.

Kylie Hicks:

Kirk always knew how to make me laugh. He always came to my sports events to cheer me on and tell me to keep my head up when something went wrong. I'll never forget him, and think of him every time I step out on the track.

Terry Mikel:

I remember Kirk because of his basketball skills, his friendliness, and how happy he always was. He helped me in grade school on my basketball skills. I thought he was a better coach than Coach Milam. I didn't really know him but he was always nice to me. I will never forget him.

Danny Chapman:

He was a great athletic role model!

Shannon Satterfield:

In the eighth grade Kirk, myself, and the rest of the class were in P.E., playing basketball. I was standing on the sidelines when Kirk ran over to me. He kept looking down at his jersey number and saying, "It's falling off." Suddenly, he ripped the number off and handed it to me. "Keep this, it will be worth money when I'm famous," he said. I always believed he would and that's why I still have it.

Frank Gibson:

My fondest memory of Kirk is the Saturday he, Grant, Mike, and I went to the state finals. It was a great day going to the morning games spending the whole afternoon with him and then going to the championship game that night. It was already a great day, but it being only a week before he died made the day just more special. That was my fondest memory of Kirk.

Becca McConnell:

KIRK

So here we are thinking about him
And our future days are looking
grim.

Lightning flash in the sky and
Moments later his soul was flying
high.

Now he's left us to face our grief
and

He can be in heaven to feel calm serene relief.

So keep his memories strong and alive
And in our hearts he'll never die.

Unsigned:

I remember the time I saw him in the gym shooting hoops. He had on the expression of pure happiness. The world is a sadder place without the light of Kirk to guide us through the treacherous paths of life.

THE LETTERS

As I said, my family and I received a number of letters as well as other correspondence after Kirk passed away—some only days after. Handwritten letters appeared more often than anything typed—a mark of the times I suppose, before the internet and e-mail came to dominate our personal exchanges. I'm happy to share some of these letters. They, too, reveal a breadth of thoughts, feelings, and words of consolation and support.

We were propped up by these letters when things got pretty rough. As I've said so often since then, I do not think I have the words to adequately express how much I appreciate the care and attention taken by those who wrote Diana and myself. I thank those who offered their prayers and encouragement to Kirk's sister and brothers, and to those people who've made up our extended families over the years.

Let this be enough of an introduction.

Joshua Bush:

> Dear Gentrup Family,
>
> I wish to send you my love and support, now, in your time of need.
>
> I am a friend of Kirk's. I say am, rather than was, because I feel that he is still with us.
>
> I feel that I speak for everyone who knows him when I say, "We all loved him and valued his friendship." Kirk was a "one of a kind" type of person, whom will be deeply missed.
>
> If I had to describe Kirk in one phrase, it would be from a song because it seems as though he lived his life by this phrase, "I don't try

anything, I just do it." I say that because in many cases trying involves giving up, but Kirk never gave up. For that, I will always admire him.

I can't say that I know exactly what you are feeling, but I can say that I have a good idea.

Eight years ago my little brother was killed. I was there and saw it happen, but there wasn't anything I could do to prevent it from happening. At the time I didn't think the pain would ever go away. After a while the pain did, but memories of him never did and never will.

I know that Kirk is now walking with Christ. And I know that we will one day meet again in heaven.

I think that we (his friends) have learned something, that is to "hold on to what you have and appreciate everything, because nothing is forever. Love and support are the two strongest weapons ever conceived, and with them we can conquer all."

I pray for you daily and hope that God helps you to gain strength and courage to face another day.

I hope that this letter shows how much I love your son. He was a great friend. I know that I wasn't his best friend, but I also know that he valued every friendship. The things about Kirk that will always be remembered by me and all of his friends are his smile and laugh.

I wish there was some other way that I could give you support, but writing is all I know.

I made it through a great tragedy, and I will support you in any way possible to help you overcome yours.

Love,
Joshua J. Bush

P.S. "Jesus said, 'I am the resurrection and the life. He who believes in me, though he may die, he shall live. And whoever lives and believes in me shall never die." – John 11:25-26

Barb Harrison:

There are no words that could be said to help lessen the sorrow and sadness you are feeling. As a mother of a sixteen year old, my heart goes out to you and I think it actually breaks for you. There is not one day, that sometime during the day, I think about this. I guess my own child is a constant reminder.

I remember when he first met Kirk at Fountain Central at a camp. He came out with a piece of paper with Kirk's phone number and address on it. My son, Cort, was so excited because he had a met a new friend. He wanted to stay in touch, write, and call Kirk. I don't think they ever did, but I know Cort would always say that he talked to Kirk when ever Fountain Central would play North Vermillion. He also talked about the talent Kirk had for basketball. That is also Cort's favorite sport so he is always looking for good talent in the other players. He caught onto Kirk's real fast. I've seen Kirk play and heard others talk about him and you have every reason to be extremely proud.

Both Monday and Tuesday's articles in the newspaper brought tears to my eyes. I go to the church and I have faith, but there are just so many questions. And I know it is not for us to question. I envy the strength you have shown and the acceptance of God's will. I have often heard it said that when we walk through our earthly gardens, we do pick the wilted and dying flowers to get them away from the pretty blooming flowers. But we pick the good flowers because of their beauty in our eyes. It's the same when God walks through the garden of life.

He takes out the old and the dying ones, but he picks fresh blooming ones, also. I can only believe that it is as you say that your son was hand-picked by God. That would have to be the "ultimate" of all our earthly accomplishments. I just don't know why something so wonderful has to hurt so bad and cause so much heartache and sorrow. I do not know you and you do not know me. I had just felt I had to express my feelings and I'm sure there are many, many others feeling the same way. You are in our thoughts and prayers daily and I'm sure many others' also. That has to be a comforting thought to know so many people care and are thinking of you all.

I know what memories get stored up in sixteen years and that is something no one can ever take from you. Keep all those memories close to your heart and they will always keep Kirk around. God gave us memories so we could have roses in the winter. Cherish yours. I pray that God will watch over you and your family during this time and the days to come.

Barb Harrison

Tom Bookwalter:

April 13, 1995

Dear Cruiser,

I'm Tom Bookwalter, Charlie's father. I don't know you, nor did I know Kirk, but feel as if I do through all that Charlie has told me. I wish not to intrude in your time of grief but I feel compelled to write. Please excuse the use of the computer for such a personal note—my handwriting is poor and clarity important. The message is no less personal.

Cynthia, Charlie's mother, and I are so sorry about Kirk's death. I'm not sure what anyone can say to provide thought for comfort for when anyone dies so young the injustice is too real, the understanding so very, very hard. It is times such as this that reinforce my belief that there must be a grand plan about which we know nothing and have no control, only the faith to believe that things happen for a reason and, hopefully, not in vain.

It is impossible to convey the depth of my sadness...I shed tears along with everyone else at the service on Tuesday, not only for Kirk but for you, Diana, the rest of your family and for all who will suffer his loss. From all that I know, Kirk was such a special person. His zest for life, belief in his family, his faith in all that was good are things that we who remain can use as an example for all the time we have to give here on earth.

I want you to know how much I enjoyed the eulogy you gave for your son. My heart ached for you as you stood before all of us there and spoke so eloquently, without bitterness for what had happened, but with love for a young man who touched so many lives in his too brief time among us. You asked that Kirk not be forgotten. I assure you that he won't, so long as there are those left who were fortunate to have been graced by knowing this unique individual.

I realize that this is none of my business, but never one to "mind my own business" I will continue on. Charlie told me that you have chosen not to continue coaching and I can certainly understand why. However, I sincerely hope, for your sake and that of the team who has benefited from all the talent you have to offer, that you will reconsider. From everyone with whom I have spoken about you, they have all said how much you love what you do with the ball team. And, you command a great deal of respect from the boys. Perhaps, after a bit of time has passed, your grieving process will be helped by going back to the team and doing what you do and know best. Hearing what I have about Kirk, I know he would give you the same counsel.

Charlie, Cynthia, and I wish we could do or say something which would assuage your sorrow, but all we can do is express our own and wish you all the happiness and joy that Kirk would want for you and your family if he were here.

Sincerely,
Tom Bookwalter

Dr. Ronald Hand:

Dear Ken,

This is one of the hardest letters for me to write.

We didn't know of your tragedy until we returned home from our vacation.

Many people don't know how you feel. I do know...somewhat. I lost a son (age two) in 1970. Worlds can't express the low—depressed hurt that we go through.

Be strong...do what Kirk would want you to do.

It's a big void in your life—time will heal the wound a little.

My thoughts are with you.

Your friend,
Ron

Vickie:

Dear Diana,

Flowers are so beautiful because of their vibrant or soft colors and their sweet and special fragrance. Also because they are fresh, delicate, and with us for such a short time.

I witnessed your strength at Kirks' funeral and your support and comfort of Pat and the many others mourning the passing of your son. I couldn't bear to come by the casket again because I have such fond memories of Kirk at his freshest and most vibrant. I'll always remember him holding up the play signal to his teammates as he dribbled the ball down the court to set up the offense. I'll always remember the twinkle in his eyes and the smirk on his face when we'd talk about my Katie or something they were both in at school. I especially cherish the memory of his young boy's chatter as he talked with us all the way home from Terre Haute the night the car broke down when he and his two buddies were going to the West

Vigo volleyball game. He made Dave and I smile.

Although Kirk might not have especially liked flowers at his young age, I'm sure that someday he would come to appreciate or at least understood their beauty. I hope this flower will always remind you of the freshness and vibrancy of your son's life.

His joy of life and unabashed dreams will always be with those he touched. In your heart and ours he will always be at his brightest, freshest, and most vibrant peak.

Love,
Vickie

Ron and Joanne Ellis:

Dear Ken and Family,

Ron and I were saddened by the recent loss of your wonderful son, Kirk.

We know first-hand what is like because of our only son Lance's tragic accident (1991). So you were in our thoughts from the start. We cried and prayed a lot for our sons, because they are loved and missed by many.

I don't know if you know us or our son, but he, too, was an honor student and three-sport athlete at SV. I know some students from North Vermillion did come to see us.

My husband, Ron, has always coached Boys Club, Little League, and Babe Ruth, so there's a possibility you two have passed each other somewhere.

For us, we still go day by day, because there is no pain that can touch the loss of a child. Everyone deals with grief in a different way. People so many times that have not walked in our shoes try to give "well-meaning" advice, but they have no idea what we go through.

We have found that it does help to talk to families that have had similar experiences. So if at any time you would like to talk to us or visit we are here for you. You can cry around us, you can talk about your son—we will always listen, be compassionate, and concerned.

I teach sixth grade in the SV corporation, and Ron works at Lilly. We're not home a lot, but we have an answering machine.

Call anytime, we'd love to meet your family.

Enclosed is a check for your son's scholarship fund. We also give $1,500-$2,000 a year scholarships to students—one for athletic and one for scholastic. It's a nice way to keep our son's memory alive.

Thinking of you,

Ron and Joanne Ellis

Mandy K. Dollitt:

April 11, 1995

Dear students and faculty,

I wanted to let you know how sorry I am to hear about your recent loss (even though you don't know me). I am a senior at Georgetown-Ridge Farm H.S. and even though I did not know Kirk, I am close to the family of Damien Williams. I know the pain you all are going through and I pray the Lord be with each of you as you take things one day at a time in beginning your healing process. You're in my thoughts and prayers.

Sincerely yours,

Mandy K. Dollitt

Kristy Haase:

Dear Students,

My name is Kristy Haase. I am a junior at Bismarck-Henning High School. I heard of the loss of your classmate, Kirk Gentrup. I did not know Kirk, nor do I know any of you. However, we have something in common. I recently lost a friend to a car accident. Her name was Andrea Robbins. Her death was one of the hardest things I have ever had to deal with. There are no words that I could say to comfort you. I just wanted you to know that you are in my thoughts and prayers. Just know you are not alone in this. I understand the pain you are going through. There isn't a minute that goes by when I don't think of Andrea. I find comfort in knowing she's being taken care of. I also know she'll take care of your friend Kirk. I know this is a very difficult time and I just wanted to express my deepest sympathy.

Kristy Haase

The Lesniaks:

Dear Ken and Family,

Please excuse the length of this letter but I just had to express the positive impact Kirk and you have had on our family, which you probably would have never known. Your friendly gestures have gone further than you could imagine.

Over the years the few times that Stanley and I have had the honor of talking with you and Kirk were good and impressive encounters. Your courtesies and positive attitudes always stood out, but what dominated our meetings was the atmosphere of true friendliness and caring. We always left our conversations with Kirk and you feeling better than when we started.

I cannot imagine a better indicator of a person's quality than their innate ability to convey good feelings onto others, which is exactly what your son and you did. Stanley really respected Kirk and that is not easy to do.

Good young men like Kirk don't just happen. They require a good role model that acts right rather than speaks. Kirk was a true compliment to your parenting. We all miss him and ask that you accept our deepest condolences. We would be honored to call you our friends if you would allow that.

Sincerely,

Dave, Stan, and Maxine Lesniak

Karen Turner:

May 11, 1995

Dear Pastor and Becky:

I have wanted to write this for about a month, but I guess I just needed to step back and take a breath before I could put it all into words. This letter is a testimony (which I don't think I could say in public) of what has happened in my life since the sudden death of one of our students at North Vermillion (Kirk Gentrup).

One Saturday night, the night of his death, I came to the High School to help in whatever way I could. Most of the time, it was just holding students and letting them cry. Some of the time it was consoling, some of the time it was plain reasoning.

Over the weekend, I knew that I had to prepare myself mentally for what I knew was to come on Monday. I prayed several times, for the students, parents, and for guidance, when I knew that the really tough "why" questions would come on Monday. I wasn't really sure what I was going to tell them, except a sermon kept coming to mind that I had heard when I was a teenager.

Monday morning came, and it was rough. I had several students seek me out. Two of which asked me direct God questions, and with tears in my eyes, I replied with the sermon, and I told them about the sermon, and how it might not make sense now, but it might in a month or so after the awful hurt was a little less.

The sermon was probably titled "Be Careful What You Ask For," but the gist of it went like this. A woman in the late 1800s had a son who was very ill with pneumonia. The doctor had been to her house several times during the course of a week, and the son still became worse. Finally one afternoon, the doctor came out of her son's room and told the mother, "I've done all that I can do, your son will not make it through the night. I would advise that you call your minister." The woman did call her minister, and she prayed without ceasing that God would spare her son. The mother knew her Bible very well, and used Luke 11:9, "And I say unto you, Ask, and it shall be given you, seek, and ye shall find; knock, and it shall be opened unto you." By the morning her son was better, and ended up surviving the pneumonia. Ten years later the mother buried her son, he had been hanged for bank robbery and murder. At his funeral, in tears, the mother said, "I should have let God have him the first time."

I explained to the students, that that did not mean that Kirk was going to get into serious trouble, because, I truly do not believe that Kirk was the kind of student to turn 180 degrees, and go into the opposite direction, but I didn't know what his future held, but God did. It could be a tragic accident or a horrible disease. The students seemed happy and pleased, and understood what it was that I was trying to tell them.

A couple of hours later, I was talking to one of the coaches, and told him what had transpired, and how I explained it to them. After I told him about the sermon, he shook his head, and said, "Isaiah 57:1, 'The righteous perisheth, and no man layeth it to heart; and merciful men are taken away, none considering that the righteous is taken from the evil to come.'" I was consoled myself, and I really think that the coach was as well. (I was also surprised to know that this coach knew his Bible as well as he did.) This experience that we went through showed me how many people I work with that are Christians, but because of the law, unless a student asks us specific questions, we are not allowed to explain our point of view.

On Tuesday, one of the students I told the sermon to came back to my office, with a smile on her face. She said, "Karen, you know that sermon you shared with me yesterday?" I told her that I did remember. She said, "I've been telling it to a lot of my friends here in the school, especially when we have trouble trying to understand. She said everyone thinks it's the neatest story. It's so good to have an answer to something like this; no one else could give us an answer."

Pastor, I have no idea how many students heard that story, and I suppose I never will know. But how such a tremendous blessing for me came out of such a tragedy, I'll never know. These kids here are good kids for the most part. There are too many that are messed up, and have problems, and there are times when you feel like throwing up your hands and saying, "I've had enough," but with education there is a bug that bites you, and you can't turn your back on these students, no matter how upset you get.

I also feel that some of those students probably told one of the local ministers about that sermon. Because about the time I thought I was about to be able to take short steps ahead, I received a letter from a local minister, thanking me for all my efforts to help any of the students who had had a hard time dealing with Kirk's death. What amazes me is that in only telling a few students, it was like a newspaper being printed on how the story made the circuit.

The reason for this letter is so that it can be used again, for some reason. God has laid it on my heart to type it. I have no idea how far this letter will spread, but you have my permission to use it in any way that would encourage another individual. I figure there has to be a reason why every night I tell myself sit down and put it on paper. So I have done that now, and I may send a copy to Kirk's mom. I'm not sure yet. God will have to lead in that one too.

God bless,
Karen Turner

Pamela "Drue" Hawkins:

JANUARY 25, 1996

My Dearest Friend Kirk,

If I could talk to you one last time, there would be so many things that I would thank you for. Before I ever met you, I knew of the boy with the pink hair who had the Batman sign shaved in the back of his head. You were the boy that thought about basketball instead of girls. I knew before I met you that you were special, but little did I know that those were not the things that made you special.

When we first started being friends was when we had study hall together in the 7th grade. I always looked forward to that hour because I knew you would have something interesting to talk about or something to do. Like the time you made me write that love letter to Grant to pay him back for something or when we tied people who were sleeping's shoe laces to their chairs.

I wonder why they never put us in study hall together again?

The only reason I was involved in student government was because you talked me into running for President and then you refused to run for Vice President because you would not be below me. You ran for treasurer and I never did quite understand that. We had so much fun in Student Government and the seminars were always fun. I remember one in particular, we were standing in a gymnasium with hundreds of students we didn't know and all of a sudden out of nowhere a ball hit me right in the face. You laughed so hard I forgot about the pain and just got mad at you.

I have so many precious memories of Mr. Harper's class and Art in 10th grade and this has nothing to do with learning.

I love to think about the talks we had about our futures. I loved to hear you talk about basketball. How you wanted to start varsity as a freshman and play at I.U. for Bob

Knight. You told me you would pay a million dollars to hear Bob Knight scream at you to play better defense. You always had everything planned out and I never once doubted that you would accomplish your goals. You were not only my "coolest guy friend," you were a wonderful role model.

I now know that everything you have done here has paid off in heaven. Even though I know you are in a wonderful place, a selfish me wants you back to make me laugh instead of cry, to watch my games and tell me what I did right and wrong, to be a friend to people who have made mistakes. I miss you more every day and I wish you were here telling me stories about Darby and Scott's gorgeous girlfriend.

You are a wonderful person and the best friend I could ever ask for. I look forward to the day that we will meet again in heaven. I'll wait patiently if you promise to greet me.

THANK YOU KIRK FOR BEING SO WONDERFUL AND REMEMBER I LOVE YOU AND MISS YOU.

LOVE,
DRUE

Carol Smith:

To: Coach Corey and the baseball team:

I am writing you to share some things that I feel needed to be said to you as Kirk's friends and teammates.

My name is Carol Smith. I am Kirk's Aunt, Diana's oldest sister.

I have been watching with interest in the paper the games you have been playing since Kirk's death. I know it has been so very difficult for you and I do understand.

But knowing Kirk since the time he was born into this world and watching him through the years, he would want you to set your goals high and take care of business.

We loved him so very much and from a baby to the young man he was on April 8, we never saw him give up. Kirk set very high goals, was disciplined as a player and a person, practiced long hours, and played the game with everything he had within himself.

He was and is a winner, never a quitter. I really don't think Kirk knew the meaning of giving up, he always reached deep down inside to try to win the game. I realize when you take up the field you think of Kirk and rightly so, but that memory of him should stir something up on the inside of you to cause you to play your very best (the way he always played).

I see you have his initials on your caps and the patch with #13 on your sleeves, which to me means you are honoring him. So if you are going to give true honor to him then go out and win for him. He would not want you to give up, because that was never a part of him.

Kirk knows and we as his family know you love him and miss him so very much.

I would like to encourage you to think about how Kirk would want you to play the ball games or how he might handle a similar situation. He would want you to play up to your abilities, because he was a winner, and also to set high goals, for you see, that is how he would handle it.

Sometimes in this life we are dealt tragedies; we don't understand why. I believe they are sent to us to see how we will deal with it and to see what we are made of. Will we be defeated or will we turn it around and look within ourselves, pull ourselves up, and go on?

That's what Kirk would want, us to go on. Knowing that Kirk was a fine Christian young man and having lived his life as an example of a Christian, makes it a little easier for his family to bear this because we know he is with the Lord Jesus.

Kirk gave you a wonderful example of how a young person can make it without drugs, alcohol, tobacco, or any other thing that would destroy your life.

So, what you need to do if you truly want to honor him, then live your lives to the fullest with your God-given talents and give your lives to the Lord above and then someday you will see Kirk again.

God bless every one of you and I pray for you.

Kirk's aunt, Carol Smith

Josh Paddock:

Dear Mrs. Crowder and Mr. Gentrup,

Once again, I would like to thank you for the scholarship that you awarded me back in 1998. Not a day goes by when I do not think of Kirk and the impact he had on my life. I remember the unselfishness of his character in everything he did. I remember his dreams that he had for you two, his mother and father. They were not selfish dreams, but dreams of helping his family and others. When I was younger, I played basketball with him. It was amazing how unselfish he was and how he made everyone around him feel great about themselves. Kirk was never one to talk about himself, he only lifted up his friends and teammates. He gave credit to everyone around him, leaving himself out. Kirk was definitely the most amazing basketball player I ever played with. More importantly though, he was the most amazing friend I have ever known. Even though I did not grow up with Kirk, he made me feel as though I could trust him with my life, and I know I could have.

In case you do not know by now, this year I was drafted by the Philadelphia Phillies. The reason I am writing this letter to you is because I feel as though Kirk is one of the main reasons why I am where I am at today. Kirk has impacted my life in many ways that will be with me for the rest of my life. For this, I want to thank you for your son, and know that he is still with us every day. I have decided to give my signing bonus this year back to Kirk. He has been a blessing in my life, and I owe him greatly.

Thank you and God Bless,
Josh Paddock

MESSAGES AMONG STONES

I wanted to close with two pieces of writing that were left in the cemetery on Kirk's grave. The first is a poem that Chrissie Crowder wrote about Kirk. The second was left by a soldier.

TO KIRK WITH ALL MY LOVE...

If I had only known it was our last
walk in the rain

I'd keep you out for hours in the
storm

I would hold your hand, like a lifeline to my heart

and underneath the thunder we'd
be warm

The Kirk Gentrup Story

If I had only know it was our last
walk in the rain

If I had only know I'd never hear
your voice again

I'd memorize everything you said

And on these lonely nights,

I could think of them once more

And keep your words alive inside
my head

If I had only know I'd never hear
your voice again

You were the treasure in my heart

You were the one who always stood
beside me

So unaware, I foolishly believed

that you would always be there

But then there came a day when I
closed my eyes

And you slipped away

If I had only known it was my last
night by your side

I'd pray a miracle would stop the
dawn

And when you smiled at me, I
would look into your eyes

And make sure you know my love
for you goes on and on

If I had only known, If I had only
known

The love I would have shown

If I had only known

A SOLDIER'S LETTER

This letter was left on Kirk's grave. Kirk's aunt Carol found it and about a week later, while walking, ran into this person up at the cemetery. He stopped her to ask if she knew anything about Kirk. She informed him she was Kirk's aunt and all about his death.

This soldier told her of his problems and said he was searching for a friend and had ended up at Kirk's grave. He didn't know how or why he ended up there. It just happened the "small token" inside the letter was his Purple Heart.

Carol told him she knew Kirk would want him to keep his Purple Heart. It was so special. He thanked her and I know he'll never forget Kirk. Who knows? Maybe now Kirk might be his guardian angel. Someday maybe we'll know for sure.

Below is the text from that letter:

I came to find a friend, and found you.

6-30-96 9A.M.

Kirk,

What way did God call you home? Car accident? I did not know you, but it is obvious you were special. You left behind many undone things. I pray that you are at peace. I know that you are. We all wish we had people that loved us as much as your family and friends that you left behind. My only prayer is that you smile down from heaven on us all this. Please accept this small token.

C.E.M.

Ft. Hood Texas, U.S. Army
C.E. Martyn Jr.

NOT AN END

There were other letters and notes from cards that I would have included here but I considered the selections I made to be fairly representative of what the others conveyed. So many people expressed their condolences, their sympathies, and their love that I do not wish to underrate their effect on us all as a family.

Everyone wanted to bear our grief with us, to mourn with those who mourn. I am thankful to God for both neighbors and the kindly strangers that have entered our lives along the way.

CHAPTER FIVE

Death's Door

"You dream of sons or daughters who go through life and create things that are good. You see those kids go through life, and this is one of them. No one in this school disliked the boy. He identified with 450 students (in grades 7 through 12). Students idolized him, and as his friend and his principal, I can't say enough for this boy. I've known him since his birth, and nothing makes it any easier. He was just tops. He did things right. His family taught him well, and he learned."

~Oren Sutherlin, principal, North Vermillion High School

In March of 1995 my grandmother was in a nursing home in Vevay, Indiana. She was ninety-nine years old and we were all hoping she could live to be one hundred. She was born on Christmas Day so she only had months to go. We had always called her "Mother" because she didn't like to be called grandma. When I was growing up we went to see here nearly every Sunday. We would have a big family meal and my aunts, uncles, and cousins would all be there too.

I still remember how my grandmother reacted when her daughter, my mother, died at the young age of forty-eight. Then I remember when my aunt passed away at the age of sixty-three. My mother died when I was in the seventh grade and my father followed a year later. Both had died of cancer. It was my aunt and uncle, Kittie and Kermit Newell who raised us three kids from the seventh grade on.

I remember my grandmother saying, "It's just not right that a child pass on before their parents." I have talked to many people who have lived this nightmare and believe me, it's true! It's a heck of thing to have in common with someone. It is a fraternity I wish no one to be a member of. Speaking for myself, I can't imagine anything being worse. I think people grieve in different ways. I grieved by talking, writing, and helping to set up the scholarship fund. I also tried to comfort others.

I think everyone who has lost a child has something in common. They all know something of what that person feels. No one knows exactly how they feel. The impact of the loss of a child affects families in so many different ways. I can only speak from my own heart. My first thought was, "How could we go on without him?" I constantly had to remind myself that I had so much to live for, especially Dale, Deena, and Kaleb.

(Did you know that Kirk was the one who picked out Kaleb's name?) There was also my new granddaughter, Darby, the beginning of our next generation. Her name was taken from my mother's maiden name, Flora Mae Darby. This made my grandmother so happy.

When you lose a child you must find reasons to live. You have to look to your faith, family, and friends. That's what I did and I found many reasons to go on. Never feel like you can't talk about it. Never feel like you can't think about it. Losing a child is not right; it's not fair, but it happens. You have to live with it and try to make something good happen from it. Make yourself do this. Ask for help if you need it.

My grandmother never lived to be one hundred. She died that March at the age of ninety-nine. I took Kirk down to see her just before she passed away. I remember her telling Kirk that Mother loved him and would be watching him to make sure he would be a good boy. I remember Kirk hugging her goodbye knowing it would be the last time he would see her alive.

When we left my grandmother, Kirk began to ask lots of questions about death. Some I could answer, some I could not. When someone ninety-nine dies it's not so hard to explain. My grandmother died shortly after our visit. At her funeral, I remember sitting there, looking around, and wondering who would be the next to die. There were a lot of elderly people there. I couldn't, not in my wildest dreams, think that the next one would be Kirk. Less than a month later Kirk was gone.

* * *

I often think that Kirk had a premonition of death. He never let up on the talk of death after going to see Mother, and especially after her funeral, it almost seemed like we talked about death as much as we did basketball, which was highly unusual. He wanted to know everything about it; where you go, how it feels, your soul, your body, faith. I mean we touched all the bases. I was glad to learn after his death that he did read his Bible to the extent that he wrote down verses and I feel maybe he did have a good understanding of death.

There were a few other peculiar circumstances that make me believe that he had a premonition. I was told by Crystal Howe that the night before our baseball tournament Kirk was shooting basketball in the gymnasium. He spent such a large amount of time doing this, a lot of time with me. At any rate, Crystal was rebounding for him on this particular night. She told me that after he was finished shooting they were sitting there talking and Crystal asked Kirk if he was ready for the tournament tomorrow. Kirk's reply was no, he wasn't ready. Crystal questioned him on this saying you're always ready for competition. Kirk was probably the most competitive person any of us knew. Crystal pressed him further and then Kirk admitted he had a funny feeling about the game, like something bad was going to happen. Crystal laughed this off thinking he was only teasing. I think he told her, "Laugh if you want, but I'm serious."

Another oddity happened that same night. After shooting basketball Kirk had a date with Crystal's sister Brandy. They had only been dating a short time. I learned of this story at Kirk's visitation. I was told by a friend of Kirk's named Courtney Hawkins that he had to put three dollars in Kirk's coffin. I asked why. He said Friday night at the movies he had borrowed three dollars from Kirk. He told me if anyone needed money they always went to Kirk because he always had money. He said most kids probably never paid him back. He told me that when Kirk handed him the money that night he held onto it tight and looked him in the eye and said, "If you don't pay me back I'll haunt you the rest of your life." He said he still held the money tight and said, "I mean it." Courtney said, "The way he looked at me...I really do think he meant it. I'd never had him do that before." Courtney put the money in his casket and I don't think Kirk ever haunted him!

The morning of the baseball tournament Kirk showed up at his sister Deena's house very early. She asked why he was there so early and he told her he wanted to hold Darby. She had fast become his pride and joy. Later Deena told Kirk he'd better get going or he would miss the bus. Deena thought Kirk was acting odd, coming by their house early just to hold Darby. Deena told Kirk he could see Darby at the game, but he said he just wanted to hold her a while longer. Kirk nearly did miss the bus and when he said he got to school he told us he had to dunk the ball one last time. We went in the gym and all he could find was one of our practice baseballs. He picked it up, ran it, and dunked it. Then he looked at us and said, "One last dunk. Let's go." I never thought anything of this at the time. After he died, his teammates went into the gym, found that ball, and wrote on it—*last ball dunked by Kirk*—and placed it on his grave. Deena still has that ball in her house in a Plexiglas holder. It's one of her most prized possessions.

* * *

Our family weddings have all included Kirk. When Deena got married Kirk was in her wedding. Unfortunately, this was the only one he would live to see, although we felt his presence at all of those that followed. My sister Betty has two daughters, Michelle and Deidre. They both included Kirk in their wedding parties. P.G.'s children, Brian and Kelli, included him too. I remember crying through these weddings mainly because of Kirk's absence.

I think the hardest one was Dale's wedding. It was held in Catlin, Illinois and Kirk would have been his best man. Dale's stepbrother Scott stood in as best man. The church in Catlin had windows around the top of the church that let light shine into the sanctuary.

I remember that Scott became ill during the ceremony and had to leave the altar. Just as he was stepping down, the sunlight came through the window to shine where Scott had been standing. It seemed remarkable—and strange—because it had been a rainy day up until this point. It was as if Kirk was standing there in the place of Scott. It was though he was saying, "I'm Dale's best man and no one else is taking my place."

I think Kirk was present at this wedding and all the others. Even after death Kirk still influenced many of his friends and family on decision they had to make.

CHAPTER SIX

Lawrenceburg

"The only things that give me some consolation in all this is that he went quickly and he's definitely in Heaven, because I think he was handpicked by God. I really believe that."
~Ken "Cruiser" Gentrup

I was born and raised in Lawrenceburg, Indiana, located in the southeast corner of the state, bordering Ohio and Kentucky. I still have many relatives and friends in Lawrenceburg and the neighboring towns. In Lawrenceburg, I am known by everyone as *Cruiser*. I've had this name since birth. Apparently my dad got me instead of a boat—true story. I didn't even know that my real name was Kenneth until the first grade when the nuns insisted on calling me by my given name.

Fairly often, my family and I would take trips to the area to visit. When my children were young they would always go down to my brother's house to stay a week or two each summer. My P.G., his wife Paula, and children Brian and Kelli lived in Rising Sun, Indiana, a town just down the river from Lawrenceburg. We were always a close family, frequently vacationing together in places like Florida and Washington D.C.

Kirk would often take his white scooter to Rising Sun so he could ride around town with his cousins. The kids always had a lot of fun while managing to stay out of trouble. One of Kirk's ways to pass the time when we went back home was to sit in the truck or van and spin a basketball on his finger. When he got tired he would put the ball on another finger or go to the other hand. It was like a contest to see how many miles he could go without stopping.

I remember Kirk being the sort of person that could be all things to all people. I was amazed at how he could relate to or talk to just about anyone, old, young, male, female, black, or white. I can remember a time in Rising Sun when Kirk was playing ping pong in Pee Wee Curry's basement. (Pee Wee was P.G.'s father-in-law.) If you didn't know any better one would think there were two little kids playing downstairs. They would be arguing, yelling, and doing their best to win. The funny thing about this is that Kirk was probably about ten years old and Pee Wee was sixty. It didn't matter because both wanted to win. Pee Wee's words to me when he learned of Kirk's death were "I truly loved that boy."

* * *

Growing up in Lawrenceburg, I had a nice life. We moved from Cook Avenue in Lawrenceburg to Greendale when I was in the first grade. Greendale was kind of like a suburb of Lawrenceburg, which was itself a town of about eight to ten thousand people. My first friend in Greendale was named Bill Cook. Bill lived across the street. We remained the best of friends growing up and still are to this day. Cookie, as I called him, came up to watch Kirk play basketball in high school. Generally, some of our other friends would come along. They knew he was going to be a good one. They also came up to his funeral. They, along with others from Lawrenceburg, attended the gym dedication.

The reason I'm writing this is I want to mention something that happened down there that was really a show of respect for Kirk. There had been so many standing ovations, those that were clearly for Kirk and not me. However, this situation had more to do with silence. After Kirk died I went back home to Lawrenceburg a lot. I found comfort there from family, friends, and also getting away. The first time, I went back I found Cookie in a bar in Lawrenceburg having a beer with some friends. The bar was packed and noisy. When I walked in you could have heard a pin drop. Everything got quiet. I could see the tears in people's eyes. Everyone started hugging me and patting me on the back. I thanked everyone and told them that I was okay and that they should go on and have some fun. At that time, it got loud again and everyone went on about their business. It amazed me that even here, in a bar, people showed how they felt about my plight.

I've always considered myself to have three best friends from my childhood: Cookie, Mike Kreinhop, and Gary Strunk. Cookie was two years younger and Snips (Mike) and Chunk (Gary) were in the same class. Mike and his wife were among those who attended Kirk's visitation. It was especially hard to find words to thank them for coming. Gary later actually got mad at Mike for not calling him so he could come there too. We later vacationed together and it helped to be with old friends and talk about Kirk.

Lawrenceburg was always a fun place for us to visit. The same was true of Rising Sun. We received so many cards, flowers, and scholarship money from this area. I can still visualize myself walking into the gym for Kirk's funeral and two of the first people I saw were from Lawrenceburg, my cousin Pam and Aunt Peg.

Later, when I coached the girls' basketball team, I would take them to Rising Sun and stay at my brother's house. His basement was like a recreation center with a pool table, jukebox, couches, games, and movies. He even had a lake to fish in and paddleboats. My girls loved going down there. We would play three or four games against other schools in the area, take the girls to

Kings Island, and hang out at P.G.'s house. His basement also contains many mementos of Kirk.

When I took the team back home to play Lawrenceburg one summer, the local newspaper was there. The headline for the story read, "Cruiser Comes Home." I thought this was pretty neat, but my first thoughts were always about Kirk. I wondered about how proud he would have been of me and my teams. I just know that my girls would have adored him. Several actually won Kirk Gentrup scholarships. I'm sure these awards were among the one they were most proud of.

To this day, I still find comfort in visiting that town. I still talk with old friends. I often told Kirk that no matter how successful you are, you should always remember your roots and always come back and give to your community. Several of Kirk's scholarship recipients have later sent donations after they started their adult lives and became successful. Lawrenceburg will always be home to me, the place of my roots.

CHAPTER SEVEN

Kirk's Sanctuary

"Kirk epitomized the qualities each student-athlete should strive to obtain: he was unselfish, enthusiastic, dedicated, trusting, intense, intelligent, self-motivated, a leader, a teammate, and a friend."

~Kirk Booe, North Vermillion basketball coach

While it is something that was obvious to anyone who knew Kirk, the importance of the gymnasium in my son's life can never be overstated—or talked about enough. I can't begin to calculate the hours we spent in the gym at North Vermillion High School. As I've said elsewhere, the gym was Kirk's home away from home. It was truly like a sanctuary where he could go to be focused and empty his mind of everything but the ball, the hoop, and the shining floors beneath his shoes. It was also the place where he could shine his brightest, aglow with the bright light of talent and dedication.

He spent more time there than anywhere else. He was lucky I had keys to the gym and he took full advantage of that fact. If he couldn't find enough people to go play he would have me take him to the gym and lock him inside. I would leave and come back later to pick him up after a few hours. He was the ultimate gym rat. Even when we traveled he took his basketball with him and did workouts wherever we went. We would either find a gym or he would work on his game outside.

Every Sunday evening I would open the gym from 6 to 8 p.m. Kirk would get up, go to church, go home, and either swim or mess around for a while. He would shoot ball at home, my house, or at the gym, if I would take him. Then he would go to the AAU practice from 2 p.m. to 4 p.m. and head over to the North Vermillion gymnasium. He would get aggravated if he was late or got beat and had to sit out a game. We would play game after game every Sunday. When it got late and some were ready to quit for the evening it was always Kirk who would say, "Come on Dad, just one more game." Naturally, he would always get enough guys to play just one more game.

Throughout the week, we would have the gym open almost every day after school to get in some more play time. My friend Michael Kirchoff would bring kids over from Danville, Illinois and play quite often. His son Adam would bring his teammates and we had some pretty good games.

Adam's teammates were mostly black kids and Kirk loved this because it made for better competition. Kirk typically played against kids or adults that were older than him. He liked this because it only made him better. We always had enough people that if your team got beat you had to wait awhile until you played again. So the games were intense and Kirk hated to lose and have to sit.

I remember laughing fairly often during those open gym sessions because a lot of the adults would take it as a challenge to play against a young kid like Kirk. They would work their butts off to beat him but just couldn't get the job done. It was always in good fun. Yet it was also always an intense competition. Kirk made it a learning experience for himself.

I used to credit myself as being a pretty good basketball player. But I think Kirk started beating me before his freshman year. I could still beat him up physically on the court, but he could out shoot me and had far more speed and agility. Like I mentioned before, Kirk spent so much time working to develop his speed and dexterity. Those strength shoes were a tough workout, but also Kirk's favorite. His philosophy was to always work the most on the things you liked the least because those would be the things you were weakest at. It's easy to be good at something you like. It's hard to make yourself good at something you don't like since it generally takes more work and dedication. As such, he worked on the hardest, most physically demanding drills the most often. He thought this was the only way he would become the best player he could be. His dedication to training was ritualistic.

I feel, and I know many others felt, that he was destined to be the best or at least one of the best basketball players to come out of North Vermillion. He was on track to become the all time leader in points and assists as well as other statistical categories. He took a lot of pride in his free throw shooting. He got that from me.

He was so dedicated to his workouts that he kept charts and actually punished himself by doing pushups or sprints for missing free throws. His ball handling drills were very intense. He was almost like a magician handling the ball or spinning it on his fingers. Through hard work Kirk became fluent with either hand, making sure to give equal time to both hands during his drills. It was there in that gymnasium (and other spaces like it) that Kirk perfected the sort of skills that made him comparable to "Pistol" Pete Maravich.

I remember Kirk bringing Winston (or Winnie as he called him), his Boston terrier, to the gym with him when he shot ball. He taught the dog to bounce the ball off his head into a Fisher Price basketball goal. Kirk's patience and determination extended even to something like training that dog to do tricks. I smile when I think about Kirk pointing his finger at that dog then saying, "Bang!" Winnie would lay there motionless until

Kirk would tell him to get up. When Kirk would swim in the pool Winnie would run in circles around the pool while Kirk was in the water. He would alternate between hopping over the diving board running under the board. The whole time he would be watching Kirk. If Kirk hollered "help" Winnie would dive into the pool and take him by the arm and try to pull him out. The reason I pointed these instances out was because I want to show you how determined Kirk could be to accomplish any task he set his mind to doing. He kept at it until he got results.

* * *

When Kirk shot ball in the gym there was always somebody rebounding for him, sometimes a girl, sometimes a boy. Kirk would always buy them a pop or they would buy him one. After his death, kids were always leaving change on his gravesite and I asked some of them why they did this. They told me it was so Kirk could buy a pop. I always took this money and buried it at his gravesite.

Another thing I'll always remember about Kirk's use of the gym was that he always left the net hanging. This is when you strip the nets and they are left hanging on the rim. This was like a trademark for him. The coaches and teachers told me they could tell if Kirk had been in the gym because the nets were hanging.

We used to get a big kick out of Kirk when he would come out of the locker room into the gym walking on his hands. He had participated in gymnastics for two or three years when he was in early grade school. He could still do all of those moves like flips, cartwheels, and he had amazing balance. I always thought this helped his strength and made him a better basketball player. He never totally quit using gymnastics.

* * *

One time when Arkansas Little Rock was playing at the University of Illinois I took Kirk over for a workout. Kirk was in grade school and he got to shoot layups with the college team. He then began to shoot free throws and the college players stood around and clapped and counted as he made one after another. Of course, he thought this was pretty neat.

As a two or three year old, I took Kirk down to Evansville to the Mideast Regional to see Oklahoma play in the NCAA tournament. We went to the hotel where Oklahoma was staying. Wayman Tisdale, who was Oklahoma's star player, was bouncing Kirk on his knee. Kirk asked Wayman why his skin was black. Wayman laughed that big laugh of his and smiled his big smile and told Kirk the sun shined differently on him.

THE GYM DEDICATION

When I told Diana to make sure we could have Kirk's funeral in the North Vermillion gym I knew this was the natural thing to do. After all, it was only fitting that his final hours on this earth were spent in that gym. He had worked so hard to be a great basketball player. He was so proud to wear the N.V. uniform and that is why I felt it was only fitting that he was buried in it.

Even through Kirk died on a baseball field wearing a North Vermillion uniform, everyone knew he spent most of his time in the gymnasium working on his basketball game or representing North Vermillion in a game. That's why most people wanted the gym to be dedicated to him. At first, it was just the voice of popular opinion, but after some time, an agreement was reached to officially dedicate the North Vermillion gymnasium to my son, enshrining it as a memorial to him forever. It was a process that took most of the first year following Kirk's death.

There were board meetings and other discussions held in that period in order to address any lingering negative opinions about the dedication, but it was eventually approved. A ceremony was held on January 26, 1996 during a home game against Covington. In the days leading up to that event there was this air of excitement mixed with the solemnity of what would be happening that night.

Once again there was a tremendous turnout. Probably over two thousand people, many of them fans of Kirk. I know that night I saw a lot of Kirk Gentrup tee shirts. I think we would have had a sell out that night but all the other schools had games that night and kept a lot of people away. This was the first game that any of us (Kirk's family) had attended. People had told me that crowds had been sparse at the games, so the crowd that night made me realize once again how much Kirk was loved and admired. These fans of Kirk were not going to let him die in their hearts or their minds. He was still very much a part of their lives.

Our athletic director, Jim Puckett, told us if none of us felt we could speak then he or one of the other coaches would. I knew it would have meant a lot more coming from one of us. Even a prepared statement read by someone else would not mean as much. So I ended up speaking on behalf of the family.

Mr. Puckett began with the ceremony by retiring the basketball #4 and the baseball #13, the numbers that Kirk wore. They are permanently retired and will never be worn by another North Vermillion athlete. A huge bronze plaque with an image of Kirk dedicating the gym to him was hung in place beside one of the doors.

This dedication was very hard. It was a very nice ceremony, one that will be remembered for a long time. The newspapers and television were there to cover it. Somehow, I found the strength to get through it all. I think when you talk about a young man like Kirk, you could talk all day but I got it down to around five minutes.

While I spoke I think you could have heard a pin drop, but before and after I spoke, I entered and left to a standing ovation. I acknowledged that I knew the ovations were for Kirk, for he was the true hero this night.

I saw and talked to many people that night that I hadn't seen for a long time. My brother and his family came from Rising Sun to attend the ceremony. Also, my sister and her family came from Atlanta, Georgia. Friends of mine from Cincinnati came also, all fans that had come to watch Kirk play.

Below is the text from the speech I gave during the gymnasium dedication.

> I would like to open tonight by borrowing a phrase from Lou Gehrig. Tonight Kirk's mother, Diana, and I consider ourselves to be the "luckiest people on the face of the earth." Lucky because the good Lord blessed us with a son like Kirk and allowed us to keep him for 16 years. Lucky, also, because of the honors that are being bestowed upon him here tonight.

Everyone here has their own special memories of Kirk. Some of you remember him as a classmate; some remember him as a friend, a teammate, a confidant, a boyfriend, or a role model. We, as a family looked at him as a loving son, brother, grandson, cousin, nephew, and uncle. But, we also looked at him as a role model. Even though he was only 16 years old, we looked up to him and admired him. We admired his hard work and dedication to whatever challenge he took on. All of us here were always proud to have known Kirk and to have him as a friend or relative.

Even though we only had him for 16 years, he provided us with a lifetime of memories. I don't think that I, as a father, or Diana, as a mother, will ever utter the words that we were ashamed of Kirk. He always represented our family, school, and community well. Diana said at the Beef House dinner that many of you here witnessed Kirk's death, but many more of you witnessed his life, and that is what is important. I think these words say a lot about Kirk.

I can remember standing out in the hallway with Kirk and Kirk pointing to the jersey of Mike Newell, and saying to me, "Dad, someday there will be another jersey in there—mine." Tonight that becomes a reality, and I know Kirk is smiling down on us all saying, "See, I told you so, and my baseball jersey too—Dad, this is just awesome."

Kirk's career here at North Vermillion is now left to the imagination. What might have been, could have been, or would have been, we can now only dream about. The papers said that Kirk had the potential to be one of the best ever at North Vermillion. This also was one of his goals and with his dedication; I have no doubt that he would have accomplished this. He set his goals high and worked hard to accomplish them. We don't feel that there will ever be a more dedicated basketball player at North Vermillion, but we hope there will be many more like Kirk, boys or girls who are totally dedicated to their family, their game, their friends, coaches, and teachers.

We also want to take this time to thank the good people of North Vermillion, the Wabash Valley, and surrounding areas for everything. After Kirk died, there were so many flowers, cards, phone calls, and so much food. We were very touched by everyone's concern. We had no idea that Kirk had touched so many lives. Even today, we still get occasional cards from people who write so many nice things about Kirk and say how much they miss him. His gravesite is always covered with mementos from family and friends, and many people tell me they think about him every day.

We want to thank Dave and Barbara Erwin, for they are the reason we are here tonight. Also, all those who worked so hard to help the Erwins work toward this gymnasium dedication—you were the true supporters of Kirk who made all this possible. Coach Booe, I'll always remember something you said to me when we talked about Kirk. You told me if you could have a son, you would want him to be just like Kirk, not just athletically, but as a person. You said you wouldn't change a thing. Hearing comments like that makes us feel that God had some really special purpose for Kirk. Someday, we hope we will understand.

There is a trophy case now in the hallway with many of Kirk's mementos, pictures, and awards. We want you to look at this case and plaque and remember what Kirk stood for and how well he represented this school and community. With the dedication of this gymnasium to Kirk's memory, his name will live forever here. The annual scholarships in Kirk's name will help others to further their education. The scholarship fund will continue to grow, and thanks to the many generous contributions received, has reached nearly $39,000. Also donations have been made to the Cayuga Christian Church in Kirk's name, and nearly 50 Gideon bibles have been placed in Kirk's memory. We hope you all continue to feel Kirk's presence here, and keep your memories of Kirk alive. He always made us proud of him, and so now let's make him proud of us.

I often wonder if maybe Kirk didn't know more than the rest of us. I remember him saying to me, "Dad, the next two years, this team is mine. I'll take the freshmen under my wings and we're going to work hard and be better than anyone expects us to be. The freshmen he was talking about were this year's sophomores: Grant, Jeff, Mike, Frankie and the rest of you. He told me he would never leave you guys alone. I believe that you are under his wings and he is always with you, cheering your every move, applauding your every basket. Every time I saw Kirk, the first words out of his mouth were, "Let's play ball, Dad," or "let's shoot some hoop." So now I close by saying to our North Vermillion team from Kirk—Let's play some ball, fellas. Play as hard as you can, for as long as you can, and make us all proud.

We love you Kirk, and we miss you.

So now a plaque hangs on the wall as you enter the gym. A case holds his retired #4 basketball jersey and his retired #13 baseball jersey, as well as many of his awards and mementos. This was, is, and will always be Kirk's gym. I don't think anyone will ever spend a bigger percentage of their life in it than Kirk did.

Kirk flying high

Kirk running the ball

Kirk with Drue Hawkins

CHAPTER EIGHT

Time Marches On

"As a student he was all a teacher could ask for. He was concerned about his grades and worked hard to make the best grades he could. He also enjoyed himself in class and had the ability to make others enjoy school. He had the ability to lighten up a room with his presence."

"As an athlete he was competitive and worked hard at making himself and his team better. I coached him two different sports and in both sports he wanted to make our team the best it could be."

"As a person there was none better. Great sense of humor that would make people around him feel better and at the same time keep everyone on their toes. He shared all of his qualities with classmates and teachers. He will be sorely missed, but never forgotten. I thank God that I had the opportunity to know him."

~Don Corey, North Vermillion coach

In the year that followed Kirk's death, it seemed like everything I did reminded me of him. People kept saying it would get easier with time, but it only seemed to get harder. His friends and coaches still came by to visit and talk. I know everyone just missed him so much. His classmates and teachers said that there is this emptiness at school that refused to be filled. It simply wasn't the same without him there. I know, like me, many people visited his gravesite practically every day for a long time, sometimes leaving mementos and notes, while other times simply coming to talk.

I drove by the cemetery everyday on my way to work. Every day I told Kirk I loved and missed him. For the next year or more, I visited his grave daily. I never missed a day. It became a big part of my life. Although I knew intellectually that he was now with God, I still could not help but feel closer to him there than anywhere else. Sometimes I stayed only for a few minutes; other times maybe an hour or more. The way I looked at it was if Kirk were here I would have been spending a lot more time than that with him playing basketball.

His grave was always decorated nicely. Most of these mementos and notes were left anonymously. I knew he was visited quite often by friends and relatives and even strangers occasionally. I knew this because we would clear his grave and in no time, the grave was covered again. I knew that he was still an inspiration to many people including myself.

* * *

After Kirk's basketball and baseball jerseys were both retired, I started seeing the numbers four and thirteen a lot. Kids were wearing them on clothes, shoes, hats, more. When I went to Rising Sun to niece Kelli's volleyball games she would wear the number four in honor of Kirk. The same was true when I went to Kaleb's basketball games; he wore the number four too.

I had a hard time keeping up with all of the expressions meant to kindle the flame of my son's life. Not only were there patches on players uniforms or numbers kept on their persons, but there were other more elaborate gestures.

For an AAU basketball tournament that was held in Kirk's memory, the association had tee shirts printed for it. The shirts had Kirk's name on them along with the caption "We will never forget." Originally, one hundred shirts were ordered and then more had to be ordered. I believe at final count around a thousand tee shirts were sold. Our grade school even had a day each week where everyone wore their Kirk Gentrup tee shirts. They showed up quite often around Eugene and Cayuga, as well as other surrounding towns too.

The N.V. sports program had a full page dedicated to Kirk. Our year book also had a page dedicated to Kirk. I ended up resigning my coaching duties. It became too difficult to attend any of the athletic events. To me, I guess Kirk was North Vermillion, and North Vermillion is just not the same without Kirk.

* * *

I can only speak for myself but I do have views on how some were affected. As for myself, I lost my youth, the kid in me, that day. Kirk was the one who kept me young. He was the one who kept me in shape, playing basketball almost daily. I was coaching, running, and always attending games usually with Kirk. I lost all of that with one bolt of lightning. I feel I began to grow old on that very day. I don't know how many hours were spent by Kirk and I in the gym or how many miles we ran up and down that court, but it all ended that day.

You can certainly say that my life before Kirk's death consisted mainly of playing basketball—and I mean lots of basketball! The only basketball I played during that first year was a Gus Macker Tournament in Danville. I only played in this because I had promised someone I would play. I thought about Kirk the whole time we played. We won three games and lost two so we did okay, but I still think we would have won if Kirk were alive. I would have definitely been in better shape and Kirk would have been there cheering me on. Basketball used to be my life but not any longer. I still love the game but it's not any fun without Kirk.

I stayed away from the gym for the longest time, not stepping foot inside until the dedication of gymnasium. Now others open it up for kids to play. Every Sunday night I kept thinking of how I should be up at the gym playing ball with Kirk. It hurt even to talk about or watch basketball. I was always left with this ache in my gut and wondering what Kirk would have done or how he would have handled a situation in the game. I think I related every moment of my life to my son. I kept asking those "what if" questions. My mind would not rest.

THE SCHOLARSHIP FUND

It became clear to me early on that I wanted there to be a scholarship fund in Kirk's name. The first effort to establish one took the form of the Beef House Fundraising Dinner. Our guest speaker for that event was Indiana assistant basketball coach Ron Felling. There was a tremendous turnout for this. I would say between 300 to 350 people. We made about $4,000 which went to the scholarship fund. Diana gave an emotional talk about Kirk and also talked about the scholarship fund. Ron Felling gave a nice talk and, at times, he too became emotional about Kirk. (Kirk's dream was always to play basketball at Indiana University and I'm not about to think he wouldn't have accomplished this. He was the type of kid Indiana looks for, very coachable and very dedicated; he was also a good student.) I think Coach Felling had a very good idea what kind of kid Kirk was just by the show of emotion at the dinner.

During the dinner we had a drawing for some raffle items. Coach Bob Knight of Indiana University sent some autographed pictures. He also sent an autographed basketball. Coach Sherman Dillard also sent an autographed basketball. Dillard was the head basketball coach at Indiana State University. It was really strange at the raffle. Kirk's little cousin Kyle Dunham drew out the winning tickets. The first ticket drawn out was for an autographed picture of Coach Knight.

We ended up selling several hundred tickets at $1.00 each; I bought five of them myself. The first ticket drawn out was mine. I took the picture and gave it to my youngest son Kaleb. The next number drawn out was again one of mine. I had them draw again. Anyway, to make a long story short, by the time the drawing was over my numbers had been drawn three times, my son Dale's once (He got the Sherman Dillard basketball), and my daughter-in-law Mary Jo once. The Bob Knight basketball went to Drue Hawkins, a very dear friend of Kirk's. It was almost like Kirk was drawing the numbers himself. The evening was a complete success and I have it all on film.

My friend Roy Armes from work filmed all of it for me.

Other events followed and donations were coming in all the time throughout that year. In time, the inaugural scholarship winners were chosen. The winners from North Vermillion were a double take—the Hollowell twins. So instead of one, $1,000 scholarship begin given to NV, two were given, one each to Thomas and Terry Hollowell. They were two great kids and friends of Kirk's. I hope they still recognize how significant that moment was and what it meant. Two thousand dollars isn't too shabby! They were the first recipients of Kirk's scholarship money—a distinct and lasting honor and one I'm sure they'll appreciate more as they go on in life.

The Wabash River Conference $1,000 scholarship went to Kyle Wooten of Turkey Run High School. Kyle was all-conference in football and basketball. He was also a good kid and an excellent student. He knew Kirk and competed against him for two years in basketball. I personally think he was a good choice because I believed he was a lot like Kirk.

I swore when we started this that I wouldn't rest until we had an endowment of at least one hundred thousand dollars. We made that amount in 2007. Through a lot of hard work on the parts of family and friends, we made it. We never begged for money. We had fun events to support the effort.

BACK TO COACHING

I did end up coaching the freshmen basketball team. While coaching has always been a passion of mine, Kirk is really the one who got me into it.

During Kirk's seventh grade basketball season I was asked to coach and I did. While the pay for this was pretty good, I really did it for the sheer enjoyment, especially knowing I would be coaching Kirk. After his seventh grade season, I kept the seventh grade team instead of moving up for two reasons. The first was to better Kirk's career in basketball. He needed to know and learn other coaches and their approaches to the game. He needed to learn that Dad wouldn't always be there. I think he agreed with me on this. The other reason was I wanted other coaches to know the enjoyment of coaching a kid like Kirk. You could have talked to any of Kirk's coaches and they would tell you the same thing.

Anyway, as I said, I did end up coaching the freshman team. While it was very difficult, it was at the same time successful. It was therapy for me. I had a wonderful group of kids, kids who all knew and looked up to Kirk. I think one thing that made me go back was when I heard some kids say it was like I had died along with Kirk. Suddenly, neither Kirk nor I was there anymore. I knew Kirk wouldn't have wanted me to be this way so I went back only two weeks before the season started. I had a lot of support from the other coaches and I know I cried a lot both in private and in front of my players but everyone understood. In fact, they even cried right along with me.

I had all my practices at the grade school and I only coached the away games. My coaching friend Kory Zumwalt managed my team during the home games. I had had this team as seventh graders and I knew it was really a good group of kids and that too is part of the reason I came back. I guess you could say we kind of leaned on each other during the season. I know I talked about Kirk a lot to this team and I used him as an example quite often. I think I always will because right now he's the best example I've ever had. I think some people think that if you don't talk about it, it will go away. They almost try to run and hide from death. Not me! I'll always talk about Kirk. To me, he'll always be there, a part of these kids' lives, inspiring them to be as committed as he was.

* * *

Even after the gym dedication, it was still very hard to go to games. I did attend the girls' sectional which was held at North Vermillion High School. Some of the girls on the team had asked me to attend in person. I really didn't want to go, but I thought it meant a lot to them. Even though the girls weren't favored to win they played hard and pulled out a sectional championship. Immediately after winning the final game the girls made their ways up to me in the stands and each hugged me and said they did it for Kirk. He was their inspiration. They said they thought about him the whole time.

The boys team didn't fare as well in their sectional. The loss of Kirk was just too much for them to overcome. But, I know all the coaches, just as I did also, wondered after each game how it might have been different with Kirk on the floor. I thought of what would happen next year during Kirk's senior year. Would there have been a conference championship, a sectional title, or even a regional title? How about the college recruiting? Kirk would have actually enjoyed that. Again, so many nagging "what ifs."

During the season the team wore the number four on their jerseys in memory of Kirk. It was at this time that I really started to notice kids from other schools with Kirk's name or initials on their shoes or hats. His AAU teammates wore mementos of Kirk. Some wrote his name on things. Some wore a pair of Kirk's gym shorts under their uniform. They all told me that they had pictures of them in their rooms and they talked to him or thought of him every day. They were kids from other schools. Kirk and his AAU teammates had become a very close-knit group.

At the end of the basketball season at the athletic banquet when it came time for me to speak about my team everyone gave me a standing ovation. Once again, I knew this was all in admiration for Kirk. It seemed really odd not seeing Kirk going up to receive the free throw or assist award.

ONE YEAR ANNIVERSARY

Just a few months later, I faced the anniversary of Kirk's death. I received cards and phone calls that day. I was really surprised how many people remembered. Lots of people, let me tell you! Diana told me that all the kids at school wore yellow ribbons that day. Also they decorated Kirk's tree outside by the flagpole. The kids always kept Kirk's tree decorated for all the holidays and also on his birthday.

I stopped by the cemetery that day and I was there for almost two hours with Kirk's aunt Carol. All day long, I was told, many cars were in and out of the cemetery. Deena told me when she was up there that it almost looked like the day of the funeral. There were so many cars and people. Diana told me the same thing. I know the next day his grave was covered again with many flowers and mementos. It didn't surprise me that people remembered, but it did surprise me how many people remembered. Once again, it was an outpouring of love and affection from people showing how much Kirk had affected their lives.

The baseball team also placed a nice wreath and card for Kirk. I'm sure they think of him often during their games. Scott Hicks left his scorecard and ball from his first varsity victory in golf. He wrote on the card that he had dedicated the victory to Kirk. I thought this was especially nice so I took this card and ball and had a plaque made for him with the card and the ball mounted on it. I wish I knew who all left things on Kirk's grave so I could personally thank them, but it's just impossible to know. I save a lot of it whenever I can.

For me and us as a family, I think the one year anniversary was hard in some ways, yet almost a relief in others. I didn't really think about it again that day. I think about it every day—all the time. Yet, on that particular day I think I could look back and be relieved that I had made it a whole year. I know if there was a way I could be with Kirk again, I would do it. But, my beliefs tell me that God has a plan for all of us. His plan for Kirk was something really special. I don't know what his plan is for me but I do know that if I live according to God's plan that someday I will be with Kirk again.

When I visited I looked at Donnie's grave next to Kirk's and I realized that I might have to wait many, many years before I see him again. We felt like we missed out on so much with Kirk's potential, but I realized that Kirk would always be a sixteen year old, good looking, athletic, young man. Once again, imagination was the word. What might have been or could have been, or should have been, I can only imagine. So, the one year anniversary was both difficult and soothing to a point. So many remembered my boy. What more could I ask for?

I know when a young person dies there is much more attention paid. I also know that Kirk was no more special than any other child. All children are special in many ways. He had lived such a full life and had left such a lasting impression. As we've said so many times, he touched so many lives.

* * *

Once that the first year was past I had a lot of things to look back on. Even though Kirk was gone, my life still revolved around him. Everything reminded me of Kirk. I related everything to Kirk. I was thinking one day of everything I liked to do when Kirk was alive and I realized that while I still could find some enjoyment in them, it was in a paler less distinct way. The vibrancy and color of life had been leeched out when my son was taken.

I still liked basketball, but no longer felt elevated by it. I still liked coaching, but it felt less rewarding. These as well as other activities no longer held the same appeal without Kirk there to enjoy them too. The enjoyment I would have had with the purchase of a new car was marred by the fact I couldn't see Kirk's excitement. Even at the second annual Kirk Gentrup tournament in Terre Haute, Indiana, it was nice to see the teammates play ball, but I couldn't really enjoy it without Kirk being there.

I've been to two weddings that Kirk would have been in. I liked them, but I didn't enjoy them. In fact, cried through them both. Everything has been like this. They were left shadows of themselves without Kirk's exuberant spirit there to share in them. He enjoyed everything in life. Kaleb, Dale, and I spent a lot more time together, mainly because they missed him too. Deena, on the other hand, had Darby to help occupy her time.

* * *

There were two things I said would never have gotten in this life: an earring and a tattoo. Well, I have a tattoo. When I got it, I told myself that it would serve as an undeniable reminder of Kirk—as if I needed one. Located on my right arm, it was a picture of Mickey Mouse spinning a basketball on his finger. Kirk was written on my arm beneath the tattoo. Mickey is wearing a North Vermillion basketball uniform with a number four on the shirt. I chose this design because Kirk was constantly walking around spinning a ball on his finger. My son Dale also got a tattoo on his shoulder, a picture of Kirk. Many times, people regret getting tattoos, but I don't think Dale or I will ever regret getting these.

My locker at work was plastered with pictures and write-ups about Kirk. One of my favorites still is the article Mrs. Pence wrote about the dedication of the gymnasium. Her brother, who is a writer for the *Clintonian*, also wrote a couple of nice articles about the dedication. When I went to talk to her I felt that I could have sat and listened all day to her talk about him. I know she was devastated by his death as were many others. Drue Hawkins' mother, Rhonda, called me occasionally to see how I'm doing. She told me that Drue still had a picture of Kirk on the dashboard of her car.

I think I decided long ago that I absolutely refused to let him die, to no longer be a part of my life. He'll always be very much alive in my mind and in my heart. I hope someday all of my memories about Kirk's life and death will be passed on to Kirk's family. I hope maybe others will enjoy what I've written also. It's what led me to write this book. But of course, I'm biased. I write all of this because I want his life to always live on. That's worth the effort of my lifetime.

KIRK'S CLASS

In 1997, Kirk's class graduated from high school. In some ways this seemed to put some sort of closure on Kirk's death. I guess at times I seemed to worry that maybe at this point he might start to be forgotten. It was a foolish thought now that I think about it. His grave was still being visited regularly even two years after he passed away. Although he was probably not visited as often as before, I still saw signs that people were thinking about him. Sometimes, it made me sad for those who are forgotten. All of those lonely, bare graves. It made my quest for his immortality bitter sweet.

Like I had said often since then, the words I spoke at the gym dedication still held true. Kirk's career was left to the imagination. I think during those two years, I did a whole lot of imagining. I wondered if Kirk would have lived whether he would have been all-conference or maybe even all-state in basketball. Many have told me yes. Would he have been all conference in baseball? I think he would have been. At the time of his death he was leading the team in batting average as a sophomore.

I wonder what colleges would have recruited him for basketball, what coaches we might have met along the way. I felt that I should have been filled with excitement going to see him play college ball, but I know it will never happen. Kirk told us often that he would be an Indiana All-Star. Would that have happened? Would he have broken the high school scoring record? What do you think? How many assist awards, free throw awards, or just any basketball awards would he have won? Just imagine how many! Would he have been homecoming king? Who would he have taken to the prom? Any time a young person dies one is left with so many unanswered questions. I know I was. (We all were.)

As a team would we have won a sectional, maybe two? How about a regional? I've talked to coaches and others and most seem to think that during Kirk's senior year we might have only lost two or three games and at least been in the regional championship game. I know I was just speculating along with all of them; there was nothing else I could do.

These might have been the rewards and excitement we could have enjoyed if Kirk had lived. Today, I tend to look more at the rewards that resulted from his passing. I do believe one of the most important was the spiritual impact. The church grew noticeably after his death. I still have no idea how many were baptized and brought to Christ as a result of my son's untimely death.

During those first two years, around $9,000 was given in scholarships, some of which was matched by various colleges and universities chosen by recipients. Everyone who won seemed to treat it like a gift directly from Kirk. It wasn't so much about the money as it was about the great honor. Each one of them was deserving of that honor.

The support for anything to do with Kirk was phenomenal. Not only did we make money for the fund at a golf outing but we also made money for Dollars for Scholars. They were able to give out $3,000 in scholarships, more than they ever had before. After the first golf outing, it was decided to make the event an annual one.

* * *

At the graduation of Kirk's class Diana and I were presented with Kirk's cap and gown in a special ceremony. Even though this was hard to do it was still nice to see that he was remembered. Also so many of the students had their caps airbrushed with Kirk's numbers, his initials, even a basketball with his number on it. The 1997 year book had another full-page spread on Kirk and he was mentioned throughout the book in captions.

I now look back at Kirk's life and I see a life that was so unfulfilled but yet at the same time I see a life that, despite its shortness, was so rich. Kirk did more in his sixteen years than most did in sixty.

I see today's athletes crying about money and aches and pains and I know Kirk would have never acted this way. I know he always played just for the love of the game, just to cherish those special moments out on the court.

I don't think any of the people who knew Kirk could ever forget his laugh, his smile, or his wonderful personality. Certainly, we'll never forget his basketball abilities. My thoughts on Kirk are infinite—I could go on forever. Nothing could tarnish my opinions of my son.

I think it would be best to end this by saying, "Kirk, to me you were the best son anyone could have ever hoped for! I love you and I miss you. I will carry your memories with me the rest of my life. I will see you again."

Kirk Gentrup Memorial Scholarship Award Recipients

1996
Kyle Wooten
Terry Hollowell
Thomas Hollowell

1997
Doug Hollingsworth
Drue Hawkins
Joel Wesch
Katie Hicks
Kylene DeAth
Paul Greene

1998
Bill Marcinko
Brian Newman
Grant Erwin
J.R. McFall
Josh Paddock
Julie Bell

1999
Allison Erwin
Amanda Noggle
Danny Chapman
Gretchen Groover
Jenna Sheridan
Sarah Jukes

2000
Anne Hart
Erin Mock
Joe Bishop
Matt Booe

2001
Adam Darnell
Danny Keyes
Jessica Beynon
Kim Turner
Ryan Weir
Sarah Allen
Thad Dunham

2002
Abby Gibson
Edgar Wharton
Megan DeSutter
Sherri Norman
Tim Hicks
Travis Taylor

2003
Adam Weir
Annie Morgan
Dustin Foster
Holly Crain
Jennifer Puckett
Kayla Hinkle
Lockey Ellis
Rachel West

2004
Anna Stayton
Anne Morningstar
Brittany Crain
Karen Wickens
Lindsay Varner
Tyler Phelps

2005
Steve Hartman
Kaleb Gentrup
Tricia Tolbert
Neil Switzer
Quinn Carli

2006
Kyle Dunham
Brent Hicks
Evan Lunsford
Robert Harrison

2007
Michael Overpeck
Jordan Crain
Jenna Spencer
Sarah Lewis
Ryan Taylor
George Hinote

2008
Dennis Webb
Drew Sheppard
Erick Hill
Hannah Clingan
Kayla Conrad
Wes Fishero

2009
Heagan Smith
Ross Carli
Colin Brown
Kiernan McMullen

2010
Shane Smith
Zach Burney
Jacob Rankin
Aaron White

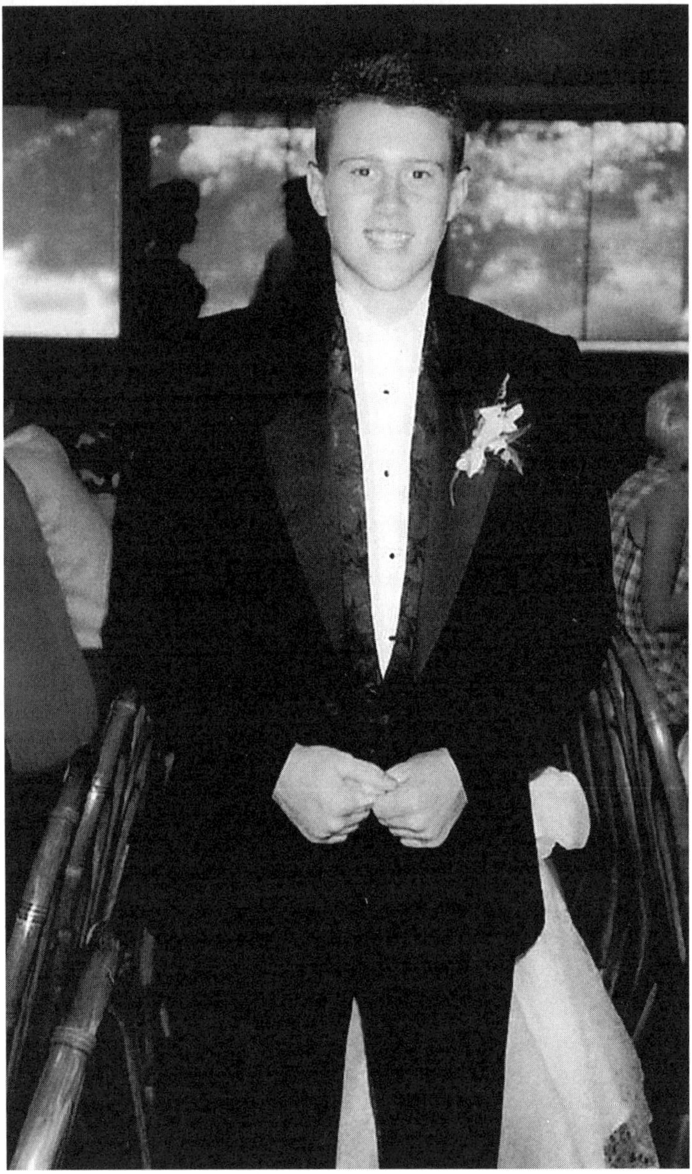

Kirk at Deena's wedding

AFTERWORD

Once I was finished writing this book, I felt that there were many things I still wanted to share, so many points I wanted to make. I hope I can accomplish both in this afterword.

I was talking to P.G. on the phone and he talked about what an "easy read" the book was, but yet so hard. He and my daughter Deena both said it was difficult to get through a few places without welling up with tears. Anyone who knew Kirk personally would understand this. (I hope any person who's lost someone special could relate.)

I hope by now that those who've read the story understand that I didn't write this book for sympathy. I certainly did not write it for recognition. I wrote it because I earnestly want future generations of my family, the scholarship recipients, and others to really have a better idea about the sort of person Kirk Gentrup was. I want people to know that no matter how bad the tragedy, how difficult the situation, there is always a reason to go on living.

I've shared my own gamut of emotions as they ran high and low. I know there were many times when I simply did not want to go on. I couldn't find solid reasons. I wanted to be where Kirk was. Still, time is said to "heal all wounds" for a reason. Yes, I went through my bouts of praying to God for comfort and help, then turning around and cursing him for taking Kirk away. I do not know how anyone can go through losing a child and survive without believing that they will be reunited one day.

At the time of Kirk's death, my granddaughter Darby had just been born; I still had Dale, Deena, and Kaleb—so much to live for. Since his death, my family has grown considerably and I often wonder what they would have thought about Kirk. This makes me realize that if I hadn't survived, I would have missed out on so many things.

I have a loving and caring wife Rhonda. Dale and his wife Mary have three children, Andrew Kirk, Lainey Elizabeth, and Evan Kirk. Deena and her husband Jr. Martin have three children, Darby Quinn, William Jerry III, and Ava Grace. Kaleb and his wife Amber have two children, Hailey Elizabeth and Lucas Alan (after Kirk Alan). My stepson Donny Gill and his wife Ramona have Eli (with baby Iris on the way). My stepdaughter Kayla Hinkle lives in the Indianapolis area. All of Kirk's step-siblings at the time of his death have all prospered. Scott Crowder and his wife Jena have two children, Hayden and Audrey. Joe and Jennifer Brewer both have done well for themselves. Jennifer has as daughter named Martha.

As I write this, thoughts keep racing through my mind, both about Kirk and about his life. I'm so afraid I've forgotten something or someone of importance. I think of when Kirk used to drive around in Junior's Tracker or his own blue Cavalier and how his uncle Denny Smith promised to let him take his "Vet" to the prom if he kept his nose clean. I think of Kirk's classmate Brad Carron naming his son Kirk and hoping we wouldn't be upset. We were honored! Whenever I see any of Kirk's neighborhood friends like Bill and Chad Johnston, Jimmy Strubberg, Chris Laws, Scott Watkins, Autumn Badger, Tiffanie Dunavan, Amber and Ricky Pasquale, or the Hathaways who lived across the street, I often think of how their lives changed with Kirk's tragedy.

There is Wendy Solomon, the young girl that sat at the visitation all night, who still contacts me occasionally in reference to Kirk. I know that she and many others kept, and still may keep, many mementos of Kirk. We passed a lot of his possessions to his friends.

I guess I could go on and on about this. There is so much more I could say. It is hard to stop, fearing I'll forget an important event. I hope people understand that every person, every event could not be talked about. By definition, this book has been limited in scope. In the end it is mostly my story about my son. Where I could, I've included what others have said (and felt) about Kirk. I'm grateful for all those who knew and loved him so much.

Diana and I are glad we have the Kirk Gentrup Scholarship. We're glad that we as individuals did not seek to profit from his death. His scholarship fund has allowed many young adults realize their academic dreams. The added benefit for us was the opportunity to keep Kirk's name—and scholarship—alive forever. This is our continuing work.

The plaque that hangs outside of the North Vermillion High School gymnasium